Shadowboxing

the rise and fall of George Dixon

Steven Laffoley

Pottersfield Press, Lawrencetown Beach, Nova Scotia, Canada

Copyright © Steven Laffoley 2012

All rights reserved. No part of this publication may be reproduced or used or stored in any form or by any means – graphic, electronic or mechanical, including photocopying – or by any information storage or retrieval system without the prior written permission of the publisher. Any requests for photocopying, recording, taping or information storage and retrieval systems shall be directed in writing to the publisher or to Access Copyright, The Canadian Copyright Licensing Agency, 1 Yonge Street, Suite 800, Toronto, Ontario, Canada M5E 1E5 (www.AccessCopyright.ca). This also applies to classroom use.

Library and Archives Canada Cataloguing in Publication

Laffoley, Steven Edwin
          Shadowboxing : the rise and fall of George Dixon / Steven Laffoley.
ISBN 978-1-897426-44-9
1. Dixon, George, 1870-1909. 2. Boxers (Sports)--Canada--Biography.
3. Boxers (Sports)--United States--Biography.
I. Title.
GV1132.D59L34 2012   796.83092   C2012-903605-6

Cover design Gail LeBlanc

We acknowledge the financial support of the Government of Canada through the Canada Book Fund for our publishing activities, and the support of The Canada Council for the Arts, which last year invested $24.3 million in writing and publishing throughout Canada. We also thank the Province of Nova Scotia for its support through the Department of Communities, Culture and Heritage.

Pottersfield Press
83 Leslie Road
East Lawrencetown, Nova Scotia, Canada, B2Z 1P8
Website: www.PottersfieldPress.com
To order, phone 1-800-NIMBUS9 (1-800-646-2879) www.nimbus.ca

For George Dixon

Throughout history, the powers of single blacks flash like falling stars, and die sometimes before the world has rightly gauged their brightness.

— W.E.B. Du Bois

Acknowledgements

I am, as always, indebted to many for helping to bring this book into being: Lesley Choyce, Julia Swan, Peggy Amirault, and Gail LeBlanc for their continued commitment to creating meaningful books; William A. Mays, editor and owner of the *National Police Gazette,* for his useful research; Deborah Goodfellow and David Wiggin for their critical eyes and open ears; Terry Chisholm and Derrick McPhee for their Prince Edward Island Green Couch Writer's Retreat; Barbara Freedman Laffoley for her contribution of rare resources; and Bernice Suitor and Emma Laffoley for their unqualified patience and support.

What follows are reflections and renderings drawn from first-hand accounts and second-hand recollections. All words quoted originate in newspapers of the day. All fights described are drawn from ringside reports.

Before the Bell

I used to be a good fighter, but I don't know what I am now.
  – George Dixon (1908)

An hour before midnight, on January 5, 1908, a yellow Taximeter Cab clattered west along East 27th Street in Lower Manhattan to First Avenue, where it turned left and stopped near the heavy double doors of Bellevue Hospital. The cab idled roughly as the driver stepped down from his high seat and opened the side door.

Three men emerged.

"George Dixon the negro ex-featherweight champion applied last night at Bellevue Hospital for treatment," New Jersey's *Trenton Times* would report the next morning. "He was accompanied by a white man and a negro."

The two men with Dixon each held an arm as they passed through the entrance doors into the reception area. Inside, they approached a low, wooden admitting desk, where the nurse on duty was seated. The nurse looked up at Dixon. No doubt, she was distressed by what she saw. Dixon's eyes were clouded, his face drawn, his skin pallid. She turned and reached for a registration form. As she did, the physician on duty, Dr. Ransom Hooker, glanced up from his desk.

He recognized Dixon.

"George," he said, "what are you doing here? Last time I saw you, you were up at the Long Acre Athletic Club, and you didn't look much in need of health then." Dixon knew the club well, a poorly lit, decrepit warehouse on West 29th Street where second-rate boxers fought in a makeshift ring for a few dollars a night.

"To tell you the truth," said Dixon, his voice weak, "I'm down and out."

Dr. Hooker's face betrayed concern. He stepped away from his desk and helped Dixon to a nearby chair.

Dixon breathed heavily as he sat.

"John Barelycorn has got me," Dixon said, "and I am suffering from rheumatism."

Dr. Hooker nodded. He turned and retrieved the admitting form from the nurse. Then he sat down and wrote Dixon's name across the top. He reviewed the questions.

"Who is your nearest friend, George?" he asked.

"Well," Dixon said, "they are mostly all gone now. But the best friend I ever had was John L. Sullivan. He's the only man that would let me have money when I wanted it." Sullivan had been the first heavyweight boxing champion and was possibly the only boxer more famous than George Dixon in his prime.

Hooker began writing Sullivan's name, when Dixon interrupted. "But he doesn't live here."

Dixon looked to the floor and fell silent.

"George," Dr. Hooker asked again, "who is your nearest friend in the city?"

"Michael Harris," Dixon said after a moment. "256 West 41st Street."

Hooker wrote the name and address.

"And where were you born, George?"

"I was born in Canada," Dixon said, "but I've been here for thirty years."

"And your age?" Hooker asked.

"Thirty-seven."

Dr. Hooker looked up and stared for a moment at the man sitting in front of him. Dixon, feeble and exhausted, looked much older than thirty-seven. Almost reflexively, Hooker offered Dixon a piteous smile.

"And your occupation, George?"

Dixon looked at his hands. They were swollen and sore. He made a fist of his left hand and turned it slowly. "I used to be a good fighter," he said, "then a teacher in boxing." He hesitated and his eyes filled with tears. He slowly looked up at Dr. Hooker. "But I don't know what I am now."

* * *

George Dixon was the finest boxer of his generation and arguably among the finest boxers ever. His accomplishments in the ring were extraordinary: the first black boxing champion, the first Canadian champion, the first champion of multiple weight classes, and the first champion to lose and regain a title. In a twenty-year career, Dixon defended his title more than any other champion – then or since – and reportedly fought in an unprecedented eight hundred bouts.

Making these accomplishments even more astonishing was the context within which these achievements were earned. In an age when black men were routinely lynched for simply being black, George Dixon publically fought and beat hundreds of white boxers across

America, Canada, and Europe. He even married a white woman.

So, too, George Dixon was a great innovator. As much as anyone, George Dixon defined what we recognize today as the sport of boxing, introducing and refining many training and fighting techniques still used more than one hundred years later. Long- and short-distance running, the punching bag, shadowboxing, and any number of combination punches and defensive maneuvers – the list of Dixon's contributions to boxing is uniquely long.

Before Mohammad Ali and Joe Louis, before Sugar Ray Robinson and Jack Johnson, before Marvelous Marvin Hagler and Sugar Ray Leonard, before all the great black boxing champions of every age and of every weight class, there was George Dixon.

He was the first.

And he was the greatest.

Renowned boxing historian and *Ring Magazine* founder Nat Fleischer once said of Dixon, "For his ounces and inches, there never was a lad his equal. Even in the light of the achievements of John L. Sullivan, the critics of his days referred to 'Little Chocolate' [George Dixon] as the greatest fighter of all time. I doubt there ever was a pugilist who was as popular during his entire career. ... [Dixon was] a marvel of cleverness, yet he could hit and slug with the best of them. He was fast, tricky, combative, canny, courageous, a master in every respect of the art of self-defense, a great ring general. His left hand was one of the best in the business. His double left to the body has never been equaled. His right was equally good."

Simply put, said Fleischer, "He had everything."

Sam Austin, the larger-than-life sports editor at America's first tabloid newspaper, the *Police Gazette* – which, more than any other newspaper of the era, helped take boxing from illegal backroom brawling to the most popular sport of the age – described George Dixon as "The Fighter Without a Flaw." In a long article, published in 1899, Austin wrote, "Even in the light of John L. Sullivan's splendid achievements in the ring, the fact cannot be disputed that the greatest fistic fighter, big or little, that the world has ever known is George Dixon."

But for all the accomplishments and adulation that George Dixon achieved and received in his lifetime, he died a beggar, in the alcoholic ward of New York's Bellevue Hospital – homeless, forgotten, and alone. It is just one of the many ironies of the complex man who was George Dixon.

Ironic, too, is that while George Dixon was being forgotten, George Dixon's archetypical story was taking hold of the public imagination – the familiar tale of a young black man who, suffocating under the weight of poverty and racism, and withering in the heat of limited opportunities, uses his fists and wits to fight his way, against daunting, unrelenting challenges, to an extraordinary reward: Champion of the World. Along the way, he grows rich and famous and is loved by all. But then, as this now familiar story goes, he overreaches. He gambles, he drinks, and he lives the self-indulgent life of the "sport." Finally, as this story requires, he stays in the ring for one fight too many.

And he loses it all.

This archetypical story – the rise and fall of the black boxer – has become cliché. Yet the rise and fall of George Dixon's life is, at the same moment, singularly different because his story was the first of its kind in modern boxing. He followed no one. He cut his own path and created his own life. For this reason, his story – his triumphs and tragedies as well as his rise and fall – transcends the cliché.

Further, the real importance of George Dixon's life story lies not in the act of boxing itself, but in how, through the act of boxing, Dixon's unique life was distilled to the essence of human triumph and tragedy. Author and boxing aficionado Joyce Carol Oates once wrote, "Boxing is about being hit rather more than it is about hitting, just as it is about feeling pain, if not devastating psychological paralysis, more than it is about winning."

Life is like that. It is not so much about winning the fight as it is about taking the punch and carrying on. George Dixon's life is compelling because few boxers in the long history of the sport took a punch – literally and figuratively – as hard as he did and carried on so well.

And even he, in the end, lost the fight.

As we all do.

So who was George Dixon and what motivated this genuinely modest man, raised in the small community of Africville, Nova Scotia, to achieve what no other black man before him had ever achieved? What strength of character earned him, against all odds, the title of true greatness? And what failure of character, in the end, took that greatness away? The answers to these questions were difficult to discern, in part, because concrete, primary-source information was so hard to come by. Though George Dixon was among the most written about sports figures in the late nineteenth century, few facts are firmly established about his life outside the ring. And though a number of biographical essays about Dixon do exist, nearly all offer notable inaccuracies and numerous distortions. As a consequence, our understanding of George Dixon has been as limited and lifeless as the cartoon image on his 1909 American Caramel Trading Card.

This book hopes to change that.

Of course, entering the ring with the elusive George Dixon often proved difficult, even daunting. For the biographer, it is no small irony that among the many innovations George Dixon introduced into the "sweet science" was shadowboxing. At times, the effort to recount the rise and fall of George Dixon's life was much like that – an artistic act of shadowboxing. Parts of George Dixon's life are often well documented, while others are missing altogether. So this biography was written as though it were a fight in the ring, as a series of hard-thrown punches – quick jabs, overhand rights, left hooks, and two-hand combinations – with the hope that what emerges at the end of the book is a rich and rewarding, word-crafted reflection of George Dixon.

In doing this, however, I must note that some words used to tell Dixon's tale are brutal and ugly. The rank prejudices of Dixon's day were unashamedly expressed in grotesque and offensive language that peppered the daily newspapers. For the biographer trying to capture both the truth of an individual experience and the truth of an age – while at the same time not wanting to offend the modern reader – this was a difficult challenge. So in those instances where offensive words were not necessary to the narrative, the words were simply dropped. However, in other instances where these words aptly reflected the brutality and ugliness of the age, and where the words were required to maintain the integrity of an important quotation, the words were necessarily kept. In the end, despite the risk of offending a reader, the narrative needs of rendering the truth of George Dixon's life were my priority.

If this biography falls short of resolving all questions raised or of filling in all aspects of George Dixon's life, then at least it stands as a far more meaningful exploration of an extraordinary man and his extraordinary accomplishments during an extraordinary time than has been offered before.

And to that extent, this book should be a worthwhile act of shadowboxing.

Part I
The Rise

Round One

I was born at Halifax, Nova Scotia, in 1870, and when [I was] about eight years of age, my parents moved to Boston. I received a public school education, having attended a Halifax school for two years. When about fourteen years of age I secured employment with a Boston photographer, and while there engaged, I first began to learn how to spar. I witnessed an exhibition one night at the Boston Music Hall, which was given by two local athletes, and the next day I purchased a book on boxing from which I gained much valuable information.
– George Dixon "A Lesson in Boxing" (1893)

In the early hours of January 6, 1908, George Dixon lay awake on his narrow bed in the alcoholic ward of Bellevue Hospital. One imagines that the ward was dimly lit and quiet at that hour, with perhaps some coughing or mumbling interrupting the silence. Almost certainly, lying in his bed and looking at the ceiling, Dixon understood that he was gravely ill, maybe even understood that he was dying.

What did he think about?

We don't know, of course. But one imagines that he gave some thought to those events that shaped his life, recalling the faces of family and friends and remembering thrilling moments in the ring. So, too, he may have recalled his childhood, when he ambled along the railroad tracks that cut their way through the small community of Africville, Nova Scotia.

It is the first irony of many with George Dixon that so little is known about his personal life despite the many thousands of words written about him in hundreds of newspapers over the years. Even the exact location of his birth remains uncertain. In a 1938 essay about George Dixon, Nat Fleischer wrote that Dixon was born at "Letson's Lane, between Gottingen and Brunswick streets, in Halifax, Nova Scotia." More than fifty years later, tennis player and author Arthur Ashe claimed Dixon's birthplace as "Leston's Lane in Halifax." Likely, Leston's Lane is merely a misspelling of Nat Fleisher's Letson's Lane, but the error says something about how the uncertain facts of Dixon's early life became clouded and confused over time. In either case, no map of Halifax shows either a Letson's Lane or a Leston's Lane in that block of the city. Then again, a small back lane in a city block that was mostly dirt and grass would not likely have warranted an official naming on a map.

Other biographical essays emphatically offer Dixon's birthplace as Africville, Nova Scotia, the small, black community within Halifax that hugged the shore of Bedford Basin, just two and a half miles north of what might have been Dixon's Letson's Lane birthplace. We simply do not know for certain. Suffice to say that George Dixon was born in Halifax, Nova Scotia, and spent his formative years in Africville.

* * *

Though Africville's exact origins are also unclear, the community is said to have begun in 1838, when William Brown, a descendent of slaves, settled on the north shore of the Halifax peninsula, overlooking the Bedford Basin. Brown was not alone for long, though. More families took up residence and soon established a community.

Eight original families were said to have settled in Africville during those years. Their surnames were Brown, Carvery, Arnold, Hill, Fletcher, Bailey, Grant, and Dixon. The first seven of these families all traced their ancestors to Hammonds Plains and Preston, other black communities in Nova Scotia. But the Dixon family ancestry was less certain, though, no doubt, they too had some family connections to the other black communities in the province. In any case, George Dixon's ancestors, and likely George himself, resided just above the railroad tracks, looking out over Bedford Basin. An 1878 map shows two lots, side by side, both owned by the Dixon family.

This small, though growing, community was sometimes called Campbell Road, and sometimes Seaview, but almost certainly, from the start, it was also known as Africville, though the name appears for the first time on a petition from 1869. The first tangible record of people residing in Africville appears in 1848, when the community formally established its church. Thereafter, in its early history, Africville appears sporadically in recorded references to city construction and land use, with Africville notably acting as the location for industrial and civic sites that no one wanted nearby.

In 1853, Rockhead Prison was built, and in 1854, the intercontinental railway laid its tracks right through Africville. In 1858, the city's "night soil" – its sewage – was located there. And in the 1870s, an Infectious Diseases Hospital was built on land just overlooking the community. Later, the city dump and a slaughterhouse found their place adjacent to Africville.

Over the years, as the northend of Halifax developed, the city council refused to provide services to Africville – no water, sewerage, paved roads, or lights. As well, they provided no playgrounds or police or fire department services. By 1954, the discrepancy between nearby neighbourhoods and Africville was stark. Noted the city manager at the time, "The area is not suited for residences, but, properly developed, is ideal for industrial purposes."

Despite this relentless racism, Africville grew to be a vibrant, close-knit community of eighty families, or some four hundred people, for more than two hundred years. Then, in 1968, in the name of urban progress, the city offered a meagre compensation of $500 to Africville families who could establish legal title to land, and then razed Africville to the ground. Today, only the railroad tracks that run outside a grassy park named Seaview, the namesake of the church that once stood there, remain as a physical reminder of the Africville community. Only recently, after years of refusing to accept responsibility for the destruction of Africville, has Halifax begun to make amends. On July 29, 2011, the city renamed the Seaview Park land Africville Park. Coincidentally, this event occurred on the 141st birthday of George Dixon.

* * *

On a midsummer's day, on July 29, 1870, somewhere in or near Africville, Nova Scotia, George Dixon was born. One biographical essay suggested that Dixon was the son of a black mother and an itinerant, white British soldier (which was the cause, claimed the essay, of newspapers referring to Dixon as a "mulatto"). But nothing beyond the statement itself supports this.

Dixon's parents were both from Africville. His mother was Maria Turner, who was thirty-three at the time of George's birth, and his father was Charles T. Dixon, who was forty-one. George had at least one brother, named James Henry Dixon, born two years earlier, on May 8, 1868. Charles would outlive George by seven years, dying on August 2, 1914. Given Maria's age when George was born, it is conceivable that George and James had other siblings.

Little more is known for certain about George Dixon's ancestry. In 1906, former heavyweight champion "Gentleman" Jim Corbett mentioned George's heritage in his syndicated newspaper column called "Corbett's Gossip of the Fighting Game." In his March 24 column, Corbett wrote, "Little credence is placed in the claim that heredity has a great deal to do with the character and nerve of a prize fighter. But in the case of George Dixon, you find an exception, which is not often spoken of. Dixon was one of the colored fighters who was never charged with being in the least bit yellow [cowardly]. It was said of him that he was the nerviest little fighter the world has ever seen. But Dixon always claimed that his fighting blood came from his grandfather, who was a white man of Irish ancestors. He did not have a drop of colored blood in him. Dixon was later married to a white woman and most always associated with white people."

Jim Corbett, like many white boxers of the age, often belittled the accomplishments of black fighters, who he routinely accused of being "yellow." When a black fighter's skill was reluctantly acknowledged, it required some racial redefinition.

That said, Dixon did appear to have had an Irish grandparent. Nat Fleischer notes that "[Dixon] was what is termed a quadroon, his grandfather having been white." Even Fleischer, who was a great fan of Dixon, was not immune to the racism of the day. When talking about Dixon's boxing prowess, he noted, "George himself was nearly white." To what degree Dixon identified with his black and white ancestry is not clear, though he was always comfortable with people of any colour or ethnic background. Of course, he was well aware of being black in a deeply racist society. And when it mattered most, Dixon always asserted his African and Africville heritage with great public pride.

* * *

One of the few tangible tales of George Dixon growing up in Africville is found in a February 1891 *Boston Globe* interview with Dixon, who was by then a boxing champion. In most interviews, Dixon said little about his accomplishments and even less about his personal life. However, he was unusually conversant for this interview, talking about both his childhood and what motivated him to become a boxer.

"This colored lad, whom the sporting men of the world are backing as a winner," noted the article, "was born on July 29, 1870, at Halifax, which is also the birthplace of his parents. When going to school, he made a practice of visiting a man named Bailey, who received the illustrated papers from the United States, and Dixon would sit with him for hours listening to stories of fights and fighters. Dixon took such a deep interest in the subject that at last he got the notion that he wanted to be a pugilist himself. After leaving Bailey's house,

Dixon would go home and for hours, he would fight imaginary opponents."

Given that Bailey was a familiar surname among the founding families of Africville, the story rings true. However, whether or not the "illustrated papers" were, indeed, the catalyst for Dixon becoming a boxer is less certain. Dixon would later offer other reasons for his interest in boxing.

We do know that Dixon spent at least his first eight years in Africville. And his story of Bailey supports his memory of Africville as a close-knit community of four hundred people. We can easily imagine George playing on the rocks near the water of Bedford Basin or swimming in the ocean on a hot summer's day. So, too, we can imagine George Dixon walking along Africville's dirt lanes, kicking at stones, or following a frog into the grass. No doubt, on Sundays, the young George Dixon went with his family to the Seaview church, where he listened in silence to the preacher or sang along with the choir. And given his rumoured return visits to Halifax over his lifetime, and his lifelong pride at being from Nova Scotia, these were likely happy years.

* * *

Sometime between 1878 and 1887, Maria and Charles Dixon moved their family to Boston. Such a move was common enough for people throughout the Maritimes, where family connections to New England were deep and the lure of better pay was strong. In 1893, George Dixon wrote in "A Lesson in Boxing," "I was born at Halifax, Nova Scotia, in 1870, and when [I was] about eight years of age, my parents moved to Boston." That said, Nat Fleischer wrote that Dixon's "parents moved to Boston in 1880." And in an 1891 interview with the

New York *Sun*, Dixon suggested that his family moved to Boston even later. "In September, 1887," the Sun article noted, "[Dixon's] father removed with his children to Boston and went to live on Knapp Street." Knapp Street still exists, a short alley of brick apartment buildings just south of the Boston Common.

Whenever the move actually took place, Dixon would remember well those early years in Boston, where he "received a public school education." It was while at school in Boston the event occurred that may have drawn him into fighting. "In the school which he attended," reported *The Boston Globe* after an interview with Dixon, "there was a fellow named Johnson, weighing about 100 pounds, who was the local bully. All the boys were afraid of him, and finally they asked Dixon, whom they had heard talking about pugilists, to fight Johnson. Dixon weighed only about 75 pounds, and was but 15 years old, but when a small purse was put up, he agreed to meet the bully. The battle was fought with bare knuckles in a barn, and Dixon won in three rounds. The fight was a fierce one, and both of Dixon's eyes were nearly closed and his mouth was terribly swollen. When he returned home he did not receive a very kind welcome, nor was he complimented upon his maiden victory. On the contrary, his mother gave him a severe whipping and made him promise he would not fight any more. Dixon would have kept that promise had his mother lived, but when she died, a short time after, his mind again turned to fights and fighters."

Though a compelling tale, this story may be little more than apocryphal or at least an amalgamation of stories, since it does not quite fit with the facts. Dixon's first professional fight occurred in Halifax, in 1886, when Dixon was fifteen or sixteen. His opponent's name was Young Johnson. The article's description of a fight in a barn seems to fit the more rural Halifax than the urban

Boston at the time. No matter the exact details, a school-initiated fight probably took place. And Dixon, who was quite small and likely the target of some teasing, almost certainly earned a reputation for standing up to bullies. And in defending himself, he would have discovered that he was pretty good with his fists.

* * *

The earliest known photograph of George Dixon was taken when he was fourteen or fifteen. It is a portrait of a young George, finely dressed in a white shirt and checked tie under a dark vest buttoned to the top. Over the vest, Dixon wears a heavy black jacket with a white handkerchief folded into the left breast pocket. Dixon's hair is neat and cut short. He looks playfully away from the camera, his head tilted slightly to his left, his body turned to the right. What stands out most in the picture is the brightness of his eyes and the warmth of his smile. The quality of the portrait suggests that it may have been taken at the studio in Boston where Dixon apprenticed. "When about fourteen years of age," Dixon would later remember, "I secured employment with a Boston photographer." The photographer was Elmer Chickering.

Chickering was born in Vermont in 1857. As a young man in his early twenties, he discovered a talent for the emerging art of photography, so he moved from Vermont to Boston and set up a studio on West Street. Not long after, he married another photographer, R.M. Wilson, and together, they built their photography business. Sometime in 1884, Chickering hired a young George Dixon to do odd jobs around the shop and then began teaching him the trade.

It was an exciting time. As the studio's business grew, it was common for local sports figures to have staged pictures taken. Baseball players, jockeys, and boxers – reflecting the three most popular sports of the day – routinely appeared at Chickering's studio for portraits. Boxers were photographed in classic fighting stances, their fists held high in front of ornate, curtained backdrops. It was during one of these sessions that George Dixon first saw a boxer. "I used to take the portraits of a good many fighters," Dixon recalled in 1890, "and I rather liked the pose and the appearance of some of them. There were others who didn't strike me as being of much account; yet I heard that they were great boxers."

The image of the boxer proved seductive to Dixon. "While [working at Chickering's studio], I first began to learn how to spar," he told a reporter from *The Boston Globe*. "One day I tossed my camera aside and went off to study boxing, and since then I've done pretty well at it. I took a notion; that's all."

These easy recollections are noteworthy for being devoid of any tangible motivation for why Dixon took to boxing. The idea that Dixon simply "took a notion" to spend his life in the ring seems playfully evasive. The thoughtful and articulate Dixon likely sidestepped the reporter's question, preferring not to explore, or at least not to share, any deeper motivations. Or perhaps he was uncertain himself as to what truly motivated him to become a boxer. What was clear, however, was that George Dixon found in fighting something deeply compelling and personally satisfying.

Not long after his taking "a notion," the young Dixon began to frequent local fights. "I witnessed an exhibition one night at the Boston Music Hall," he would say, "which was given by two local athletes, and the next day I purchased a book on boxing from which I gained much valuable information."

The only tantalizing tale that might speak to a real motive behind his attraction to boxing was the story of the schoolyard bully. Perhaps, in that hazy, apocryphal tale, there is a tangible clue or two. George Dixon was poor and black in a world where being either meant suffering. As well, he was small for his age, which may have invited painful boyhood teasing. Nothing is for certain, of course. But somewhere amid these truths – truths over which he had no control – there came the experiential alchemy that creates the burning desire to achieve greatness.

No matter the reason, however, George Dixon left his promising position at Elmer Chickering's Boston studio sometime in early 1886 and began his unprecedented life in boxing.

Round Two

How to Train: *Very few pugilists train alike, simply because where one man may be working to take off weight another may be working to put it on. I will try and explain my own method of training by saying that when I am preparing for a contest I rise about 6 o'clock in the morning and take a walk of ten miles. When I have gone about eight miles I begin to quicken the pace and come home on a good fast run. My trainers then rub me down with Turkish towels until I am dry, and then apply a wash of alcohol and witch hazel. I then put on a new suit of 'sweaters,' after which I breakfast. I usually eat the lean part of muttonchops or broiled steak well done. I eat eggs about every other day and drink Bass ale. Tea and coffee have a tendency to make a person nervous.*

After an hour's rest I start in at the punching bag and work there for about an hour. I punch the bag for three minutes and then rest one minute. I then 'rough it' by wrestling and running about until about one hour before dinner. I then go through the 'rubbing down' process again and another change of sweaters. After dinner, which consists of roast meats, potatoes and other good solid food, I read and write until about 3 o'clock. Then I go for a twenty-mile run

and upon returning am rubbed down, and another change of sweaters. Then I partake of a light supper and retire about ten o'clock. The same course is followed until I reach the weight I am to fight at.
— *George Dixon, "A Lesson in Boxing" (1893)*

George Dixon came of age when the sport of boxing was transforming from a backroom, bare-knuckled excuse for brawling to the modern, gloved, Marquess of Queensbury Rules boxing. This transformation was perhaps best embodied in the career of John L. Sullivan, who also found his life tangentially intersecting with George Dixon's in ways telling, surprising, and ironic.

Born twelve years before Dixon, in 1858, to poor Irish immigrant parents, John L. Sullivan was raised in the tough streets of Boston. At five feet ten, he was short for a heavyweight boxer, but he was tenacious in temperament as well as physically muscular and exceptionally strong in body. As a youth, he worked at numerous manual labour jobs and was known to be quick with his fists.

His professional fighting career began almost accidentally when he was nineteen. He and some friends were attending a popular vaudeville show at the Dudley Opera House in Boston. At one point in the program, an Irish bare-fisted fighter named Jack Scannell took the stage and challenged anyone in the audience to a three-round, bare-knuckled exhibition. The crowd smiled at the offer. Such exhibitions were regular features of vaudeville shows because fighting was ostensibly illegal in most cities and states. So vaudeville shows offered their patrons "exhibitions" of fistic skills.

The young, brash, and ever cocky Sullivan immediately volunteered. He dashed down the aisle and gamely mounted the stage. Removing his coat, he waved to the audience. Then he turned and smiled at Scannell, who raised his fists and postured in the familiar boxer's pose. Sullivan's smile faded as he rolled up his sleeves and raised his fists. They nodded at each other, and the two pugilists started circling. Scannell waited patiently for the impulsive Sullivan to throw a punch. When finally Sullivan did, Scannell stepped aside and struck Sullivan playfully on the back of the head. Embarrassed, Sullivan was infuriated. He rushed Scannell and punched him so forcefully that Scannell was knocked backward off his feet and into the stage piano, where he lay unconscious.

The crowed roared with approval. Sullivan had won the fight.

After that, Sullivan went on to win more "exhibitions" and moved to fighting in the ring, earning a reputation as a fearsome brawler. That said, he was not, nor was he ever, a particularly skillful boxer. Rather, he was a persistent attacker and able to withstand extraordinary punishment. "Sullivan is as fierce, relentless, tireless as a cataract," wrote sports editor John Boyle O'Reilly. "The fight is wholly to go in his way – not at all in the other man's. His opponent wants to spar; he leaps on him with a straight blow. He wants to breathe; he dashes him in to the corner with a drive in the stomach. He does not waste ten seconds of the three minutes each round."

Before long, Sullivan had amassed an impressive winning record. And though he was well known as the last bare-knuckled fighter, Sullivan had in fact only fought in four "official" bouts without gloves. Indeed, as early as 1880, he showed a decided preference for gloved fighting under the Marquess of Queensbury

Rules.[1] And in doing so, he popularized the use of gloves in the ring. At the same time, he continued to accept bare-knuckled fights until July 10, 1889, when, in a roped-off section of a grassy field before hundreds of enthusiastic fans, Sullivan fought and defeated Jake Kilrain. The fight would stand as the last bare-knuckled championship and would cement Sullivan's long-lasting reputation as a great fighter.

John L. Sullivan became the first modern sports celebrity. His picture hung in nearly every tavern and saloon in America. Thousands of fans followed his exploits in newspapers officially against the "barbaric sport" of boxing but which recorded every fight in great detail. People wanted to see him do almost anything and would pay almost anything to do so. During his reign as heavyweight champion, he found it more financially rewarding to take three years off to star in a travelling play that had been written for him than to fight in the ring.

And the fans flocked to see him.

But though he was much loved, Sullivan was also a difficult man. He was a notorious drunk, whose drinking often resulted in barroom brawls, destroyed relationships, and the loss of his health and his money. He was also a notorious racist famous for proclaiming that he would fight and beat "any son-of-a-bitch" who stepped forward – except a black man. "I will not fight a negro," he once said. "I never have and I never shall."

Despite this noxious nature, Sullivan maintained a long, meaningful friendship with George Dixon. Their lives and careers, and even their fates, seemed inexorably intertwined. "The world knows what a prejudice

---

1. The Marquess of Queensbury Rules were introduced in 1867. They were intended to refine the London Prize Ring Rules used for bare-knuckled fighting. The twelve Marquess of Queensbury Rules established the basic framework for modern boxing including a twenty-four-foot ring, set rounds of three minutes with one minute of rest between rounds, and the use of boxing gloves.

John L. Sullivan has against colored fighters," reported *The Boston Globe* in the 1890s, "but Dixon has not a warmer friend than the big fellow. Dixon did not try to gain the friendship of Sullivan, but it was the big fellow who wanted to know Dixon. Though both began their lives as boxers in this city [Boston], they never had exchanged a word until about six or seven years ago. The meeting took place many miles from here. Both were on the road with their companies and they happened to cross paths in the lunchroom of a railroad station in Pennsylvania. Sullivan had heard of the abilities of the colored lad and asked O'Rourke [Dixon's manager] to introduce him.

"From the time they clasped hands, Sullivan always had a great admiration for Dixon, and the many kind deeds that Dixon has since done for Sullivan have linked their friendship more firmly together. Whenever the big fellow had a benefit, he did not have to ask Dixon to appear. The latter was always the first to volunteer. While he could have gone to the hall and have been admitted free, he never would. He bought tickets for himself and friends and generally had to travel from Boston to New York to appear, never taking a cent from Sullivan for his work. Such acts Sullivan never forgot, and Dixon is the only colored boxer who can go to Sullivan's place and do about as he likes. He also can have half of anything the big fellow has, and there is many a white boxer that could not receive the same favors from Sullivan. When Dixon first traveled through the country with Tom O'Rourke, their route often carried them to southern cities where the prejudice against colored people was very strong, but the boxer was never insulted, for he knew how to carry himself in all circumstances."

Given their professional trajectories, it was perhaps no accident that both men participated in a three-day, three-fight event in New Orleans in 1892 that represented the true beginning of modern boxing. That event would feature Sullivan losing his heavyweight title to "Gentleman" Jim Corbett, and also George Dixon making a powerful statement about racism and sport.

But that was still years away.

* * *

While boxing was emerging from the brutality of bare-knuckled brawling, the horrific epidemic of lynching was spreading in America. Between 1886 and 1906, the years George Dixon boxed as a professional, more than two thousand black men were lynched by racist mobs throughout America. Though the vast majority of these lynchings took place in the southern United States, only four out of the then forty-eight states – Massachusetts, Rhode Island, New Hampshire, and Vermont – could claim that no black man had been lynched there.

Lynching represented, perhaps, the most horrifying act of the institutionalized racism that blighted America. By the time George Dixon had moved to Boston, the efforts at post-Civil War Reconstruction in the South had all but collapsed. One result of the collapse was tens of thousands of black Americans living without the protection of Union troops. Into this void came the Ku Klux Klan, the sharecropper system, and the Jim Crow laws that made life in black America a dangerous and often deadly challenge. Even in northern communities, black Americans were legally treated as second-class citizens. Lynching – often accompanied by dismemberment, castration, burning, and other torture – provided a terrifying means to keep black Americans in a state of deferential fear.

To be black in America during the late nineteenth century was singularly dangerous. And to be a black boxer fighting white boxers must have been nothing short of flirtation with murder.

* * *

George Dixon's first professional bout occurred in Halifax, Nova Scotia, on November 1, 1886. He was just sixteen years old. Yet, save for the date, the name of the opponent, and the location of the fight, little more is recorded. We do know that Dixon knocked out his opponent, Young Johnson, in just three rounds. It is also worth noting that Johnson never fought professionally again.

Why did Dixon fight his first match in Halifax? Perhaps it was easier to get a professional bout in the city as an unknown, and perhaps Dixon wanted the support of his friends and family at ringside as he made his first foray into professional boxing. In either case, Dixon's quick success must have buoyed his young confidence. One can only imagine the celebration that occurred that night in the Dixon home in nearby Africville.

No doubt George Dixon engaged in a number of amateur bouts in the months that followed, and no doubt his skills improved with each engagement. But Dixon was a unique fighter. More than just developing from experience, he became a true student of the sport. He spent countless hours in clubs, studying matches with care from ringside. He watched the fighters on offence and on defense. He watched their blows and counterblows. So, too, he read all he could find about boxing and worked for hours to find efficiencies in training and movement. As time passed and he learned more, Dixon seemed to acquire a rare capacity to see his opponents' intentions as if they were being delivered in slow motion.

* * *

Eight months before George Dixon fought his first professional bout, on March 18, 1886, sometime just before 1:00 p.m., sixty armed men entered the courthouse in Carrolton, Mississippi. They climbed to the second-floor room where a black man named Ed Brown was being tried for murder. Without warning, the men burst into the room with their Winchester rifles, and they began firing. "The room," reported *The New York Times*, "was completely enveloped in smoke." Bodies fell "four or five on top of each other." A stampede pressed to leave the room. Some people made for the windows, jumping thirty feet to the street only to find men waiting. Amos Mathews, for one, had jumped safely from the courthouse window only to have "the whole left side of his head blown off by one or more loads of buckshot or a Winchester rifle." More than twenty people were killed that day.

All were black.

No one was ever arrested for the crime.

* * *

Nearly a year after his first professional bout, Dixon prepared for his second at the Way Street Gymnasium in Boston on September 21, 1887. Small and light – he weighed less than a hundred pounds – Dixon had turned seventeen just two months earlier. He was set to fight Elias Hamilton, another young black boxer from

Boston who had fought and lost a single professional bout some two years earlier in Baltimore. What drew Hamilton back into the ring is unknown, but the money was good for a night's work, and perhaps he thought the young Dixon, who had no professional record of note, would be an easy opponent.

The Boston Globe reported the fight that night "was an eight-round go between two young gentlemen of color." Likely, the audience was sparse, just a collection of gamblers, perhaps, who came out to bet on second-rate fighters. Those in attendance were not disappointed. The newspaper described the bout as a "hard fight" with Dixon proving "to be the better man." As with Young Johnson, Elias Hamilton's experience in the ring with Dixon was more than enough to encourage a quick retirement.

A few years later, Dixon would remember this fight in an interview with the New York *Sun*. He recounted that he was still living with his father on Knapp Street and had been fighting in local clubs as an amateur. Another local amateur named "Sammy Cohen was challenging every bantam," reported the *Sun*.

"Dixon finally accepted his challenge, but Cohen flunked [backed out]. Then Dixon ascertained that Sandy Walker, who had agreed to fight Elias Hamilton at the Fair Play Club, had backed out. He hunted up Ed Holske, and after much persuasion, Dixon succeeded in getting the chance to take Walker's place. The sports saw that the newcomer, as Dixon was now called, knew something about fighting, and he was given plenty of chances to show all his skill by the managers of the boxing clubs of the city. Dixon became so completely taken up with the business that he visited all the boxing exhibitions given by the crack pugilists of Boston. He made it a point always to get a seat close to the stage so that he could get a good view of every blow that was given. On returning home he would practice some of the blows he had seen delivered at the show. In that way, he acquired great proficiency in his line, and it was soon noticeable that every time he appeared in the ring he showed wonderful improvement."

* * *

While Dixon was still fighting amateur bouts, a young black man named Sidney Davis was standing trial in the small town of Morgan, Texas, on July 15, 1887. Davis had been charged with assaulting a woman and was silently listening to the court proceedings when "a mob of 500 men rushed into the courtroom." The armed men ordered everyone to remain still. As one of the men bound the sheriff, the others took Davis from the courtroom "very roughly [and] marched [him] to the Basque River Bridge, about a mile away." There, at a nearby tree, the mob told Davis that he was guilty of attacking a white woman and that his "time had come." Davis began to weep. Unmoved, one member of the mob threw a rope over a limb and fixed the noose around Davis's neck. While the crowd jeered, Davis was then drawn up "to remain [hanging] until his life was extinct."

No one was ever charged with the murder of Sidney Davis.

* * *

Dixon fought yet another newcomer in October 1887, a white boxer named Young Mack. The bout was over in three rounds, when Dixon flattened his opponent with a hard right. Mack found the defeat so demoralizing that he retired from the professional ring for three years, only to return in 1890 for his second professional fight. He lost that and retired for good.

While Dixon had yet to face an opponent of genuine experience or real talent, his three professional fights to date and his numerous amateur bouts garnered him much attention among the sporting men of the city. Not long after the Young Mack fight, he was approached by a small-time manager from Boston named Young Collins, who promised to get Dixon better fights and bigger purses. Seventeen-year-old Dixon was enthusiastic about bigger purses and immediately agreed.

A month later, on Saturday, November 5, 1887, Young Collins marched into the offices of *The Boston Globe* and asked to speak with a sports reporter. When one finally appeared, the blustery Collins announced that he "would match his man against any of the 105-pound fighters." He particularly wanted Dixon to fight the talented Tommy Doherty of East Boston. "If Doherty really wants a go," said Collins, "I will guarantee a purse for a fight to the finish of a limited number of rounds, under the management of a club in this city." When the reporter asked why a fighter of Doherty's reputation would fight an unknown like Dixon, Collins responded, "Dixon has been tried and has proven he is a game fighter, one who will stand lots of punishment." Of course, Doherty felt little pressure to take on the upstart Dixon. He suggested Dixon earn a few more victories in the ring before taking on someone of his calibre.

So that is exactly what Dixon did.

* * *

The first detailed newspaper description of a George Dixon fight came with his fourth professional bout, on January 2, 1888. Dixon travelled out of the city centre, past Dorchester, into Roxbury, to fight Jack Lyman at the Earley Athletic Club on Lagrange Street. The fight "parlor" was located up "three, long and narrow flights of stairs." The room was small and poorly lit, and cigarette and cigar smoke gave the air a claustrophobic stench.

The president of the athletic club was an impresario named Colonel Thomas who had staged numerous fights in the city, usually rough toe-to-toe brawls that featured little skill and less talent. That night, after two preliminary matches – which did little to excite the patrons of the club – Dixon and Lyman entered the room with their seconds (cornermen, aids, and assistants). Dixon passed first between the ropes with his manager, Young Collins. Lyman then entered the ring, accompanied by Bob "the Black Spider" Green. There was notable excitement in the crowd as both fighters had made good names for themselves in a series of "extensive" exhibition fights. As well, both fighters had laid dubious claim to being contenders for the "105-pound championship."

The scheduled six-round bout between George Dixon and Jack Lyman – who had won his first professional fight just a month earlier – would impress those present enough to earn a good description from a reporter at *The Boston Globe*. "It is doubtful," the *Globe* reporter wrote, "whether out of the number of fights that have taken place there one could be found which would excel the bout last evening, in which the contestants were only a couple of little bantamweights, who were matched to fight six rounds."

After the gloves were tied and tested, the fighters were called to the centre of the ring. Referee Tim

McCarthy gave his instructions then sent the fighters to their corners, where they waited anxiously. The atmosphere of the hall was charged with anticipation. The bell rang, and the two fighters bolted to the centre. Dixon let fly a left jab that caught Lyman on the jaw. Lyman responded, both arms swinging. The two clinched and each delivered short uppercuts and jabs.

They broke away, circled, and exchanged light blows. Dixon threw an overhand right that cut the skin above Lyman's eye, drawing blood, then he shot a sharp left to Lyman's chin. Lyman rushed forward to clinch. After a moment they broke, and the two threw short arm punches until Lyman stepped back, allowing Dixon to deliver another left to Lyman's cut eye.

When the bell rang, the fighters returned to their corners. Lyman breathed heavily as he sat on his stool with his head tilted back. His second, Bob Green, worked the cut. "Keep away from him," Green told Lyman. "Counter with your left when he rushes. Wait for him to overreach."

In his corner, Dixon watched Lyman with a notable calm. He studied Lyman and seemed almost to know what Green was telling him. When the bell rang for round two, Dixon moved quickly to the centre and baited Lyman. Dropping his hands, he left himself open. Lyman took the hook and rushed forward, throwing a stinging right toward Dixon's head. Dixon dodged and released the trap. He countered Lyman's punch with a combination to the body and head. Stunned, Lyman began to wobble.

"You've got him, Dixon!" the crowd yelled.

Referee McCarthy turned to the crowd. "No remarks, please."

Dixon kept attacking, driving sharp blows to Lyman's nose and body. Lyman tried to counter, but the momentum was with Dixon. Lyman's eye was now swollen and closing. He was bleeding from the nose and mouth. A reporter present noted that Dixon was "without a scratch," though his "left eye was a little damaged and had begun to swell."

As the round wore on, Lyman's energy waned. He clinched when Dixon punched. Catcalls rose from the crowd. Dixon grew increasingly frustrated. "If you want to wrestle," Dixon hissed into Lyman's ear, "I'll give you all you want."

At the start of round four, Lyman found a second wind. He and Dixon stood toe to toe for almost three minutes. Blow followed blow, counterblow followed counterblow. At the bell, Lyman was "very groggy, and was very much winded." And at the start of the fifth, Lyman was lifeless. The Colonel, recognizing that Lyman had nothing left, called the fight for Dixon. As he raised Dixon's hand in victory and the crowd cheered, the Colonel was quick to announce another fight for Dixon and amateur favourite Charley Parton, in one week's time, for a purse of fifty dollars.[1]

The crowd roared.

"I can truly say," wrote the enthused *Boston Globe* reporter, "that I have seen worse fights where the purse given amounted to $1,000, and where each of the contestants had records as long as your arm."

Two weeks after the Lyman fight, Dixon returned to the ring and beat Charley Parton in six rounds, taking home the purse of fifty dollars, a sum that would have seemed like riches to Dixon. A month later, on February 17, 1888, George Dixon defeated Barney Finnegan in seven rounds. His fast rise brought him much attention.

---

1 An approximate conversion rate for a dollar in 1890 and a dollar of today is about 1 to 25. As such, a conservative estimate of $400,000 career earnings for George Dixon would be equivalent to about $10 million today. Some estimates suggest that Dixon earned as much as $750,000 dollars over his career or, in today's money, $18.75 million. In either case, such figures made George Dixon among the wealthiest black men of his day.

He was soon scheduled to fight Tommy "Spider" Kelly, who claimed the unofficial paperweight title or the "105 pound championship." But when the fight day arrived, Kelly failed to show, and Dixon easily defeated the substitute Ned Morris in four rounds.

At the end of February 1888, Dixon fought Paddy Kelly. The bout ended in a fifteen-round draw. It would be the first of many draws to come in Dixon's career, despite the fact that Dixon was often the stronger boxer. In fact, the number of draws in his record suggests something of the biases of the time. Though never explicitly stated in Dixon's fights, as a black boxer fighting a white boxer, he always faced the greater challenge. Matches that would have gone in favour of a black boxer were called a draw in order to save face for the white boxer and disgruntled patrons. As Jack Johnson, the first black heavyweight champion, would later note, "For every point I'm given, I'll have earned two, because I'm a Negro." Dixon took the draw with Kelly without public complaint.

And if he did complain in private, no record of it remains.

Dixon next fought the talented Tommy Doherty. The bout went eight rounds before it too was called a draw. Doherty was considered a serious challenge for Dixon, and the draw says much about Dixon's rapidly developing skills. Indeed, Dixon's talent could no longer be denied. Win or draw, Dixon was undefeated as a professional. And as such, he rightly earned the opportunity to fight for his first title – a match with Tommy "Spider" Kelly for the 105-pound championship of America.

That fight came on May 10, 1888. Dixon and Kelly arrived in the early evening at the Athenian Club in Boston for the championship bout. Three years older than Dixon, Tommy "Spider" Kelly was as tall with a narrow, sinewy muscularity that suggested both quickness and strength. Kelly had a habit of brushing his auburn hair up from his forehead, making his narrow face appear all the leaner. He would give Dixon his first serious challenge in the ring.

Set for seven rounds, the two fighters were prepared for a battle. "These two men," wrote *The Boston Globe* reporter present at the fight, "are probably the best 105-pound men in the business."

When the bell rang for round one, both Kelly and Dixon came out fast, with Kelly taking the lead and holding it through the second round. Dixon seemed surprised at Kelly's speed and ferocity, and spent more time defending than attacking.

In round three, Dixon was "just beginning to wake up" and effectively began counterpunching, though Kelly's "queer antics" – jumping "around the ring in great style, and by very clever ducking avoiding blows, which, had they landed, would have done much damage on the place at which they were aimed" – caused Dixon much difficulty. Yet when Dixon's punches finally connected, Kelly knew it. Said the *Globe* reporter, "The little colored boy hits like a kicking mule."

Kelly's jumping antics got under Dixon's skin. "Why don't you stand up and fight?" barked Dixon a number of times throughout the bout. Kelly, said the reporter, "responded to the call and came near giving George all he wanted."

By the end of the seventh round, the referee scored the bout even. And it should have finished as a draw, but in an effort to give Kelly a chance to win, the referee arbitrarily added two more rounds. The additional rounds settled nothing. When finally the bout ended in an undeniable draw, and most likely what should have been a Dixon win, the crowd was pleased, applauding "heartily" for both fighters. Kelly later spoke with a

Boston Globe reporter. He showed his hands. They were "badly puffed."

Given the draw, Dixon and his manager, Young Collins, were quick to co-claim the 105-pound or Paperweight Championship. Here Dixon showed a keen eye for self-promotion, particularly when it came to garnering bigger and bigger purses. And when, not long afterward, Tommy Kelly retired from the paperweight class to fight solely as a bantamweight, Dixon immediately claimed sole title to the unofficial Paperweight Championship of America.

Yet George Dixon, too, had set his sights on the more lucrative and more recognized Bantamweight Championship of America.

Round Three

The Proper Position: *The right hand is placed directly over the heart and the left arm held in a half round or semi-circle manner. The motive in placing the right hand over the heart is to rest the arm within the proper distance of the head to be raised and used as a guard against a left hand blow delivered at the face. It is also within proper distance of the waist to be lowered and used as a guard against a left hand blow delivered at the body. If the right arm was to be placed even with the waist, the body would be well protected but the face would be left unguarded.*

Then again, if the right arm was placed even with the head, the face would be guarded but the body left unprotected. You thus see the reason for placing the right hand over the heart is to rest the arm within correct distance of the head as well as the waist to stop any ordinary blow delivered at the body or face in the manners I have explained. The reason for holding the left arm in a half round manner is to have it in a position to strike a quick and effective blow. If the arm was held at full length, the blow would have no force. It would be merely a slight push.

– George Dixon, "A Lesson in Boxing" (1893)

Before 1885, boxing had no defined weight classes. As a consequence, mismatched fights were common and frequently resulted in unsatisfactory matches for spectators and serious injuries for boxers. So, too, in order to drum up interest in a bout, fighters routinely made claims to being champion of one arbitrary weight class or another, whether they were recognized by a local club or not. Spider Kelly's claim to be the "105-pound champion" was a good example. This problem persisted in part because no supervisory boxing organization existed and in part because boxing in the late 1880s and early 1890s was, in most jurisdictions across the United States, an illegal activity recognized as shadowy entertainment for gambling. As such, what mattered most in the rough and tumble of early boxing was the promotion.

Boxing then, and to some degree now, had little to do with fairness. Even after weight classes were well established, boxers who possessed a title under a given weight class would often agree to defend that title under a different weight class that naturally suited the champion's needs. For this reason, a boxer's manager was particularly important. The manager would arrange not only the fight, but also the purse. These purses would be put up by a promoter and negotiated by the fighters. At the same time, the managers and the fighters would openly offer a sizable side bet themselves. The size of this bet would often entice gamblers. And so, in the absence of an organization to designate and monitor weight classes and title fights, the tabloid newspaper the *National Police Gazette* – which had a vested interest in both boxing and gambling – eagerly filled the void, awarding championship belts as it saw fit.

In the late nineteenth century, five weight classes were established, ensuring some degree of equity in the ring. The Middleweight Class was established in

1884 for fighters up to 160 pounds. The Heavyweight Class was set in 1885 for fighters of unlimited weight. In 1886, the Lightweight Class was set for fighters up to 135 pounds. And in 1889, just as Dixon was reaching his prime, the Featherweight Class was created for fighters up to 126 pounds. Finally, in 1894, the Bantamweight Class was established for fighters up to 118 pounds.[1] Even with these established weight classes, however, fighters continued to lay claims to more specific weight championships in an effort to generate ever-larger purses.

* * *

Dixon's reputation in his early years was defined by a series of four fights with a Boston boxer named Hank Brennan, locally known as "the Pride of Boston." As with Dixon, Brennan was a fast-rising bantamweight who had made a name for himself in the amateur circuit. Though he was a serious fighter, with talent and tenacity, his first professional bout was with Dixon.

The first of the fights – a limited bout of twelve rounds – occurred on a pleasant summer day, on June 21, 1888, at Boston's Pelican Athletic Club. Given the reputations of both Dixon and Brennan in a boxing-mad city, the interest in this fight was considerable. On that day, the Pelican Athletic Club, already a popular venue, filled quickly with enthusiastic patrons. They cheered lustily for Brennan when the two fighters entered the

---

[1] Today, boxing has seventeen weight classes: Mini Flyweight – up to 105 pounds, Junior Flyweight – 108 pounds, Flyweight (also known as Paperweight) – 112 pounds, Junior Bantamweight – 115 pounds, Bantamweight – 118 pounds, Junior Featherweight – 122 pounds, Featherweight – 126 pounds, Junior Lightweight – 130 pounds, Lightweight – 135 pounds, Junior Welterweight – 140 pounds, Welterweight – 147 pounds, Junior Middleweight – 154 pounds, Middleweight – 160 pounds, Super Middleweight – 168 pounds, Light Heavyweight – 175 pounds, Cruiserweight – 200 pounds, and Heavyweight – over 200 pounds.

room and cheered for him again as the two stood in the ring listening to referee Tom Higham offer introductions.

The boxers, intent on each other, shook hands.

At the bell, both Dixon and Brennan showed caution. Each offered probing jabs and feints that missed or were blocked. When an opening presented itself, Dixon rushed forward and landed three quick blows to Brennan's head. Brennan was stunned and clinched, until Referee Higham pulled the fighters apart. When Brennan was free, he swung hard, but Dixon sensed the blow and leaned back. The punch caught air, and the two fighters returned to cautious jabs.

In the second through the fifth rounds, Dixon took the lead in action and in points. But in the fifth, Brennan took charge, offering Dixon a battery of blows. Dixon countered, leaving the flesh around Brennan's eyes swollen. And so it continued, until after twelve rounds, the referee deemed the fight a draw. Many in the room, despite their enthusiasm for Brennan, felt Dixon had taken the edge. So the referee called for two more rounds. Dixon was furious. The agreement had been for twelve. Unmoved, the referee nodded and the bell was rung for the thirteenth and then the fourteenth round. And again, the two fought to a draw. The referee claimed afterward that Brennan had the better of the fight for the latter part of the contest but acknowledged that Dixon had delivered one knockdown, which was more than enough in his mind to make the match even.

Both fighters agreed to a rematch.

They met on December 4, 1888, at the Athenian Athletic Club in Boston, where a rich $100 purse had been set. Again Dixon and Brennan fought a furious battle described by one reporter as "a hurricane." The two fought in close, with "every lead followed up" by a counterpunch. Brennan worked Dixon's body, gaining the advantage during the first four rounds. But Dixon roared back in the fifth, offering "wicked exchanges." Brennan evened the match in the sixth, "swinging his right on Dixon's ribs and getting in one or two ripping uppercuts." And by the seventh and final round, the fight was deemed even, forcing the referee to order another round, and then another. Yet, despite the tenacious fighting, neither Dixon nor Brennan could gain the upper hand.

When the fight was finally called, the bout was scored a draw.

* * *

A few weeks later, on December 22, 1888, John L. Sullivan challenged Jake Kilrain to fight for the bare-knuckled heavyweight championship under the old London Prize Ring Rules. A year earlier, the *National Police Gazette* had awarded Kilrain the dubious title of champion in an effort to draw Sullivan, whom the paper had long disliked, into the ring. Despite Sullivan's long absence, the challenge worked.

* * *

Three weeks after their second fight, on December 28, 1888, Dixon and Brennan returned once more to the Athenian Club to determine a winner between the two. Another $100 purse was put on the table, and thousands more dollars were wagered. Despite a snowstorm and bitter cold, the club was again filled to capacity with "hundreds of fans." Each fighter knew that a chance for a bantamweight title awaited the winner. No doubt, each had grown frustrated with the other as they changed their tactics with each fight in a desperate effort to find an edge.

As Hank Brennan entered the room, the referee noted that he was alone, refusing seconds. "I'll fight my own battle this time," he remarked as he met Dixon in the centre of the ring. He turned to the referee. "All I want is a square deal from you," he said. "My fists will do the rest." When the fight finally got underway, the gamblers were seen, "hat tipped, cigar held at an angle between the teeth, the hard look of the gambler plastered all over the face, and each openly taking wagers."

Dixon was favoured, seven to five.

The fight was another give and take affair, each boxer offering toe-to-toe assaults and fast-changing tactics. Dixon worked Brennan hard to the head and took the early lead, but Brennan returned in the fifth with a flurry that almost dropped Dixon. The crowd was riotous in their enthusiasm. "Hats were tossed into the air," and howls were heard with each landed blow. Yet, after fifteen rounds of arduous boxing and deft defense, the pair finished with another draw. The crowd and the fighters were furious. The referee, in fear for his life, managed to escape the club before gamblers tore him apart. The crowd then rolled into the street and, despite the cold and snow, began a riot. The Boston police were called in to disperse the mob.

Although the third fight with Brennan ended in a draw, Dixon still felt some pride at being undefeated. Between January and May of 1889, he fought Paddy Kelly, Frank Maguire, and Billy James. None of the fighters or even the fights was particularly memorable, with Dixon soundly beating Kelly and James and fighting Maguire to a suspect ten-round draw.

* * *

On the evening of January 29, 1889, Dixon was scheduled to fight Paddy Kelly, with whom he had fought to a draw in March of 1888. A small crowd had assembled as the boxers waited for their bout.

Among the spectators was a fellow named Tom O'Rourke. Barrel-chested at thirty-three with a carnival barker's savvy for reading people and making deals, O'Rourke was a few inches taller than Dixon with a thick mustache and dark hair parted neatly in the middle. He was born in 1856 in Boston and grew up, like John L. Sullivan, in the mean streets of the Irish neighbourhoods there. As a young man, he had been a mediocre boxer and later a talented rower. Now he was the owner of a café and a small local gym, and he frequented the local boxing clubs in search of talent he might manage.

That evening, O'Rourke travelled with a friend, John Blanchard, to the boxing club in Cambridge, Massachusetts, not far from the navy yard. He and Blanchard found a seat ringside, and they chatted and watched with disinterest the preliminary fights.

But when Dixon and Kelly began to box, Tom O'Rourke found his attention turning away from his conversation and toward the action in the ring. The spritely Kelly had bolted from his corner at the start and flailed wildly at Dixon with both arms. Much to O'Rourke's interest, the young Dixon responded to Kelly's attack with calm efficiency, shifting the weight on his feet and countering each rush with a sharp jab.

At the same time, as Kelly kept on the attack and landed enough blows to close Dixon's left eye, O'Rourke thought Dixon was making some careless errors. What truly impressed O'Rourke was how Dixon maintained his calm throughout the fight, holding his right hand tight to his chest and jabbing effectively with his left. Each jab landed firmly and soundly, exacting an escalating toll. In the fifth round, Dixon delivered a sharp left that buckled Kelly at the knees. Dazed, Kelly leaned backward. Dixon did not hesitate. He stepped in and struck a final blow that dropped Kelly to the canvas.

O'Rourke was intrigued. He leaned toward his friend, Blanchard. "My goodness," he said, "that would be a great little fighter if he was only taught." O'Rourke left the club that night thinking about the possibilities.

The following morning, Tom O'Rourke asked around town about Dixon. He heard that Dixon kept a room in Cambridge's black neighbourhood, so he made his way across the Charles River. As O'Rourke later remembered it, he came to the head of a narrow alley in Cambridge where he saw a stout woman leaning out from her window. He introduced himself and asked if she knew George Dixon.

"I do," she said and pointed along the alley. "He lives down the way there."

O'Rourke looked. "Well," he said, perhaps uncertain about the unfamiliar lane, "would you tell him to come over and see Tom O'Rourke?"

The woman smiled, nodded, and said she would.

O'Rourke then headed back to his gym.

Later that night, George Dixon entered Tom O'Rourke's gym and introduced himself. O'Rourke smiled and shook his hand. "I saw you fight last night," he said. "I'm thinking of taking hold of you and giving you a chance."

Dixon said nothing and looked about the gym. He liked what he saw.

"So," said O'Rourke, "what about it?"

Dixon nodded. "Mr. O'Rourke," he said, "if you handle me, I'll fight anybody in the world." He smiled and put out his hand. O'Rourke took it. The two seemed pleased at their newfound partnership. O'Rourke then took off his coat and showed Dixon the gym. As they finished their tour, O'Rourke asked about Dixon's odd habit of holding his right hand to his chest. Dixon was happy to answer.

They talked for hours.

Years later, O'Rourke would still recall Dixon's enthusiasm as he talked about boxing technique and tactics.

* * *

On June 6, 1889, Dixon was the featured fighter at the newly opened Parnell Athletic Club on 40 Kneeland Street in Boston. That evening more than two hundred sporting men gathered to admire the "well-ventilated and well-equipped" venue that could seat four hundred. The hall had the latest in timekeeping clocks, which alternated between rings and gongs to sound the end and beginning of rounds. It was said the clock cost the club more than four hundred dollars.

The evening's program offered four contests, one of which was a ten-round bout between George Dixon and Frank Maguire. However, when the time came, Maguire was a no-show. George Wright, the bantamweight champion of Canada, who happened to be present, agreed to a six-round exhibition bout. So while the crowd grew restless, Wright dressed and then, amid cheers, he entered the ring.

According to a reporter who was present, Dixon "had everything his own way from the start." Dixon struck hard and fast at Wright. Confused by the assault, Wright was unable to defend against Dixon's speed and ferocity. As the first round neared its end, Wright seemed on the verge of collapse. Dixon delivered two blows to Wright's face and then, just as Wright was turning away, offered a shot to the stomach. However, Dixon inadvertently caught Wright in the groin.

Wright was furious. The crowd shouted, "Foul!"

Wright pulled off his gloves and left the ring. As Dixon waited in the confusion of the howling crowd, he leaned against the ropes and watched the uncertain referee. Wright was soon encouraged to re-enter the ring, at which point the contest was abruptly awarded to him.

Dixon was stunned.

"In any other club the claim of foul would not have been allowed," *The Boston Globe* reporter noted, "and Wright 'gave up' when he left the ring." But the fight was recorded as George Dixon's first professional loss.

Even years later, it still rankled. "The first [loss of my career], which was to have been to a finish, was with George Wright of Canada whom I met in Boston about six years ago and he was declared the winner on a foul. During the first round, Wright left the ring three times but was induced by his seconds and allowed by the referee to return each time. At the close of the second round the referee claimed I struck Wright after the gong had sounded, and for that reason which was unfair, he gave the decision against me. I could not induce Wright to meet me again and he has many times since been beaten by men whom I have easily defeated."

* * *

To rebound from his defeat, and to maintain his status as a bantamweight contender, Dixon again fought Hank Brennan at the Parnell Athletic Club in Boston on October 14, 1889. The bout was scheduled for twenty-five rounds. Five hundred enthusiastic members of the club gathered to watch the fourth contest in the epic battle between the two well-matched fighters. This time a substantial $700 purse was promised to the winner, and again, the gambling interest and action was intense.

From the first round to the sixth round, Brennan took the lead, working Dixon's body and landing some "wicked left-handers to Dixon's face, neck, and head, and several times he uppercut Dixon in a first-class manner." As the two worked in close, it was Dixon who drew first blood from Brennan's nose.

Over the next three rounds, Dixon countered and established control, eventually closing Brennan's left eye. Undeterred, Brennan stepped up in the tenth, eleventh, and twelfth rounds.

The fight, once again, was even.

From the thirteenth to the seventeenth rounds, the edge between the fighters moved back and forth with Dixon working Brennan's bloody nose and swollen eye. In the eighteenth, Brennan landed a left to Dixon's nose, which drew blood. But still neither fighter gained a decisive edge.

In the twenty-second round, Brennan rushed Dixon and landed a sharp right and then left to his neck. But Dixon countered with a right to Brennan's head that dropped him to the canvas. Brennan was "badly dazed when he got to his feet" and Dixon continued on the attack. But Brennan clinched Dixon until the end of the round, keeping Dixon from delivering a knockout blow. Brennan returned for the next two rounds with renewed energy, fighting in close.

At the end of the twenty-fifth round, as Dixon had again established control, the club owner stepped into the ring and declared the match a draw. The referee, perhaps cognizant of the anger faced by his predecessor in the earlier Dixon-Brennan bout, forcefully objected and refused to call the match as such. The fighters' seconds then stepped into the ring and a tussle began. Finally, the crowd joined the melee until the police waded into the ring and stopped the fight.

The bout officially ended in a draw.

Boxing historian Nat Fleischer would say of the Dixon-Brennan fights, "Boxing history was made in those four battles. Never before or since has the feat been equaled." Despite the tie, Dixon had finally broken through as a respected fighter. But just being better than a white fighter was not good enough to bring victory and not good enough for a chance at the bantamweight title. He would have to work even harder. And he would need a cagey ally.

This alliance would come in a partnership with Tom O'Rourke.

* * *

Not long after Tom O'Rourke and George Dixon began their partnership in January 1889, George was introduced to Tom's younger sister, Kitty O'Rourke. Diminutive, with short, curly hair that framed her round face, Kitty was five years older than George. *The Boston Globe* would later describe her as "intelligent," "thrifty," and "shrewd" – "a pretty girl, who was considered one of the belles of the north end of Boston." As a young woman, she had many eager suitors in her neighbourhood, suggesting that she was engaging and sociable. When she began seeing George, there must have been some surprise in the neighbourhood and likely even upset. Interracial relationships, even in the northeast of America, were violently discouraged.

Yet, overcoming what must have been noteworthy hostility, the two fell in love. People would later ask Kitty why she would "cast her lot with a colored man." To the question, she just would smile and say,

"I married George because I loved him. Let the world think what it may. I will share his joys and sorrows to the last."

How long their courtship lasted is unclear, but it could not have been for more than a year. They were married by pastor Reverend Peter J. Smith, at St. Paul's Baptist Church in Boston, probably in late 1890. And for a few years, at least, they appeared genuinely happy with their lives together. One biographical essay of Dixon stated that Dixon had been married before he met Kitty, but his youth and no other corroborating evidence suggests this is not true.

In either case, George Dixon was happily married.

* * *

In late December of 1889, O'Rourke arranged for Dixon to fight Eugene Hornbacker in New Haven, Connecticut, "for $250 a side and a $500 purse." O'Rourke had been skillful in crafting the contest, declaring that a win for Dixon would be sufficient for a challenge against bantamweight champion Charles "Cal" McCarthy. The compelling tale O'Rourke and Dixon crafted took hold, and the gamblers excitedly put their money down on the fight.

* * *

Early in the morning of December 27, 1889, *The New York Times* reported, "A mob of several hundred men raided the jail at Barnwell Court House [in Charleston, South Carolina] at 2 o'clock this morning, overpowered the jailer, and took out eight negro prisoners, charged with murder … The jailer was tied and forced to accompany the lynchers. The whole thing was conducted in a very successful manner, the citizens of the town not knowing anything about it. A great many negroes are collected at the scene, and more trouble is anticipated."

* * *

On the same day, at 8:30 in the evening of December 27, 1889, George Dixon and Eugene Hornbacker entered the ring in front of an excited crowd. Dixon "wore gray tights and brown canvas shoes," noted *The Boston Globe* reporter. "The muscles on his chest, back, and arms indicated that he was in perfect trim and he had a confident expression on his face. He is a well-built lad above the waist, but his limbs seemed a trifle too small to be proportionate." Hornbacker, noted the reporter, was "stockily built and, though not a cyclonic fighter, possesses good staying powers." He "wore black tights, leather shoes and a blue silk sash." The betting was $50 to $40 against Dixon, and the action was heavy. A large Boston contingent had great faith in Dixon and happily jumped at the odds.

Dixon sat stone-faced in his corner and stared unblinkingly at Hornbacker. "I am going to do my best to win in fifteen rounds," he said to his seconds. "If I do then I will be a bigger man than Cal McCarthy, who took eighteen rounds to finish Hornbacker."

His seconds nodded.

At 8:42, the bell for round one rang, and the two fighters charged to the centre. Hornbacker led with his left, striking Dixon in the stomach, while Dixon returned quickly with a hard left to Hornbacker's face. Hornbacker staggered back and Dixon followed. The blows came fast. Four times Dixon knocked Hornbacker down before the bell ended the round. "When the men were called up for the second round," reported *The*

Evening Express, "Hornbacker was still stupid, showing plainly that he had been severely punished. Eugene tried to rally and force the fighting, but he was not in to it. Dixon was fresh and he pounded the plucky little German all over the ring and knocked him out with a well-delivered right-hander on the side of his left jaw, after they had been fighting about one minute. The fight and all lasted only five minutes."

The assembled crowd was astonished.

Charles "Cal" McCarthy, the American Bantamweight Champion, was in the crowd that night, coldly assessing the skills of his next opponent. When the fight ended, he jauntily stepped into the ring and shook Dixon's hand. "You'll be a wonderful fighter," he said and smiled.

Dixon eyed Cal with a cool stare. "You think I'm a good one, eh?" he said. "Well, you'll think so to a moral certainty when you and me meet."

McCarthy lost his smile and nodded.

The fight was on.

"Boston has a pugilistic phenomenon," reported *The Boston Globe* the next morning. "His name is George Dixon."

Dixon now had his chance to fight for another title.

Round Four

A Straight Counter: *The straight counter or 'jab' as it is more commonly termed is one of the best blows in boxing when delivered with judgment. To land a straight counter with effect, draw your opponent on to lead with his left which you stop with your right. At the same time strike out with your left, and nine cases out of ten, your opponent will be so anxious about landing his own left that he forgets to guard his face with his right and you have a good percentage in your favor of landing the blow.*

If you are fortunate enough to have a longer reach than your opponent, you need not wait for him to lead at you with his left. Carefully gauge your distance and keep your arm's length between you and your opponent, and when properly set, hit out straight from the shoulder. If your opponent should slip his head to one side and your arm pass over his shoulder, place your arm in a 'cross guard' manner against his neck or head and push him away. Always keep your eyes on your opponent's eyes and watch carefully for a right hand blow coming across your left arm while you are attempting a jab. Be sure and hold your arm still after you have landed the blow.

– George Dixon, "A Lesson in Boxing" (1893)

In the nineteenth century, the world of the boxer was also the world of the "sport" or "sporting men." It was the after-hours world of pimps and prostitutes, hustlers and gamblers, barkeeps and drunks, vaudevillians and voyeurs. Gambling and boxing were intimately intertwined and attracted their fair share of dangerous men.

"Sports" lived on the margins of city life. They lived for good times and the promise of easy money. The term "sport" began as the phrase "the sporting life," which originated in 1830 when the term "sporting gentleman" was used to describe a gambler. By the 1850s, a "sporting house" was a gambling den. The term was expanded by 1870 to include a saloon and sometimes a brothel.

Both rich and poor inhabited the sporting life, with elegant high-class houses as well as backroom places. In the saloons and gambling dens that attracted "sports," one would find a full cross-section of life – rich and poor, black and white, men and women – not found in any other part of society. Here the rigid social divisions of class, race, and gender came together in common cause and collective experience.

In the tougher sections of cities, the original sporting houses ran betting games on "dog, rat, and cock fights." After 1870, boxing became a popular betting sport in the saloons of New York's Bowery. In fact, saloons became an integral part of the boxing life – the term saloon coming into vogue in 1840 – and remained so until Prohibition. "Around 1900," notes historian Irving Lewis Allen, "greater New York had more than 10,000 saloons, and they were on nearly every street in working-class neighborhoods." With the gambling, drinking, prostitution, and general crime that gravitated around these activities, the culture of the sporting life was nothing if not dangerous.

And it was in this world that George Dixon not only pursued a championship title but also began to carve a life.

* * *

On February 7, 1890, The Union Athletic Club in Boston arranged a fight between Cal McCarthy and George Dixon for the American Bantamweight Championship. The match was to be a fight to the finish, continuing until one boxer was knocked out or quit. "Sporting men by the hundreds were present," reported *The Boston Globe*, as the two fighters entered the ring at 8:45 in the evening. Cal McCarthy was accompanied by his backer, Joe Early, and his seconds, Tom Collins and Jack McMaster; Dixon, by his seconds, Daniel Gunn and Tom McGough.

Born in McClintockville, Pennsylvania, in 1869, to Irish parents, Charles "Cal" McCarthy stood a half-inch shorter than Dixon. His hair was brown and thick and rose up in a wave from a side part. His eyes were dark and deep-set in a narrow face. As a child, McCarthy had moved with his family to Jersey City, New Jersey, where the scrappy Cal was soon drawn into fighting. He started professional boxing in early 1888. He rapidly rose to the top, with quick hands and a ferocious temperament, becoming the first teenaged titleholder in December of that year.

The two boxers on that February night weighed in at 114½ pounds each. "McCarthy," reported the paper, "looked as white and as hard as a statue, [while] Dixon [was] as lithe and strong as a young oak." The betting had been heavy leading up to the fight and leaned decidedly toward McCarthy. "Charley Johnston offered $1,000 to $5,000 even money on McCarthy," recorded the paper, "but there were no takers. Arthur Johnson, a

New York colored man, wagered $200 to $250 on Dixon, and there were numerous other bets made, such as $100 to $80 and $100 to $50 on McCarthy."

At 9:00 p.m., the fighters approached the centre of the ring where the referee, Al Smith, offered instructions and asked the pugilists to shake hands. The two then returned to their corners and to the encouragement of their seconds.

The bell rang.

McCarthy and Dixon danced cautiously around each other for a time, until McCarthy landed two quick blows to Dixon's head.

Dixon did nothing.

McCarthy struck again at Dixon's ear with his right and his jaw with his left. Dixon responded with an uppercut that fell short. McCarthy stepped in and delivered a hard right to Dixon's chest. Dixon, perhaps surprised or even stunned, backed warily against the ropes, where he stayed until the bell rang.

Rounds two and three saw Dixon overwhelmed and frequently clinching, desperate for an opportunity to strike back. McCarthy remained undeterred. He delivered heavy body blows that kept Dixon on the ropes. Dixon tried to respond, again and again, but in each instance, McCarthy tied him up.

In round four, Dixon found an opening and threw an overhand right that struck McCarthy's nose. McCarthy winced. Dixon moved forward deftly for a second punch, but the wily McCarthy slipped the blow. As Dixon followed, McCarthy countered with two quick lefts to Dixon's ear and eye. Still on the attack, Dixon picked up his pace. He moved forward and connected with combinations.

Then McCarthy struck back, pushing Dixon to the ropes with sharp combinations. Though Dixon defended well, he was unable to return blows. Again he clinched.

When the two turned together, Dixon pulled away and delivered a fearsome combination that might have dropped McCarthy had McCarthy not slipped under a right cross.

In round five, McCarthy again pushed Dixon against the ropes, delivering solid strikes to Dixon's stomach and ribs. And when McCarthy delivered another combination, Dixon returned with an uppercut that fell feebly short. By round six, betting was now two to one on McCarthy. The crowd roared as McCarthy landed blows once, twice, three times – twice to Dixon's head and once to his chest – without any response from Dixon. Finally, Dixon slipped away. Shaking off the attack, he gathered himself, lifted his hands, and rushed in. McCarthy simply danced away. McCarthy finished the round by delivering a stinging right that drew blood from Dixon's nose.

Near to the ring, the betting was now $100 to $35 on McCarthy.

Round seven saw the advantage continuing for McCarthy. Dixon struggled to find any rhythm or opportunity. He swung twice with his right, missing his target both times. McCarthy efficiently responded with blows that connected, left then right, to Dixon's head, followed by a hard left to the ribs. Finally, Dixon connected with a left to McCarthy's eye and then a left to his nose.

The heavy betting continued.

In rounds eight and nine, McCarthy worked Dixon's body. Dixon's left made a steady target of McCarthy's head. By round ten, both fighters showed serious fatigue. McCarthy was known for slowing as a fight continued, and on this night, he was true to form. Dixon soon gained the upper hand, delivering sharp blows to McCarthy's head and chest. McCarthy, in an effort to maintain his advantage, kept backing away, but

Dixon stayed in determined pursuit. McCarthy finally resolved to clinch, signalling a swing in the momentum of the fight.

Dixon took the charge.

Round eleven saw an energized Dixon delivering clean, direct strikes to McCarthy in well-delivered combinations. At one point, as the round neared its finish, McCarthy seemed stunned by a blow to the head. He dropped his hands, leaving himself open. Dixon did not hesitate. He struck McCarthy repeatedly. Only the bell saved McCarthy from a knockout.

When the bell rang for round twelve, a dazed McCarthy tried his best to hang back from Dixon, who eagerly pressed his advantage. McCarthy leaned against the ropes as Dixon attacked. The two fighters exchanged heavy combinations. Seeing McCarthy's weakness, Dixon expended great energy, desperate to finish the contest. McCarthy hung on, clinching or slipping away, only to have Dixon drive him back each time into the ropes.

Somehow, McCarthy made it to the bell.

By rounds thirteen and fourteen, both fighters were spent. They rose slowly from their corners and approached each other with caution. They circled, looking for openings and hoping for a second wind. Bets of $100 to $90 and $500 to $400 on Dixon were now offered, but none were taken, while in the ring, McCarthy offered light jabs at Dixon.

As the sixteenth round came to a close, Dixon landed a hard left to McCarthy's right eye, which quickly swelled and bled. McCarthy responded with his own blow above Dixon's left eye, which also began to bleed. In round seventeen, the two fighters found their second wind, offering clean, hard blows – but to little effect.

McCarthy's right eye bled.

Dixon's left eye swelled shut.

And the two fought on.

As quickly as it had come, Dixon and McCarthy now lost their second wind. In rounds twenty-one through twenty-three, the two offered nothing more than cautious dancing and probing with few blows landed. In rounds twenty-four and twenty-five, McCarthy worked Dixon's body and head, and round twenty-six saw Dixon deliver blows that left McCarthy's "eye and nose in bad condition."

Heavy exhaustion settled over both fighters through rounds twenty-seven to thirty-three, leaving the boxers moving about the ring warily and wearily, barely able to hold up their hands. The crowd quieted. The pugilists now seemed locked in a dance of endurance.

In round thirty-four, the tide changed. Dixon rushed forward, and the fighters exchanged damaging combinations. The crowd livened, and the betting picked up, moving toward Dixon, 100 to 80. In round thirty-eight, the two fighters were tangled in the corner, and they fell to the canvas. When they rose, Dixon delivered such a flurry of blows that McCarthy "went down to avoid Dixon's fierce rushes." According to *The Boston Globe* reporter, "The round ended with McCarthy lying on his stomach and Dixon punching at his head."

For the next eight rounds, Dixon was spent. McCarthy took the advantage, striking Dixon with powerful combinations. Yet the effort failed to finish him, and for the two rounds following, the combatants did little more than stagger. In the sixtieth round, Dixon again took the lead with effective combinations to McCarthy's head and body. And for a time, it looked as though Dixon might put McCarthy away, but Dixon could not find the final combination. From the sixty-fifth round until the sixty-ninth round, the fighters returned to staggering about in the ring, struggling to keep their arms up.

Finally, at the end of the seventieth round, after an astonishing and exhausting four hours and thirty-seven minutes, the referee, Al Smith, called the epic battle a draw.

Almost immediately, Dixon laid shared claim to the bantamweight title.

* * *

To walk along the avenues of New York during the 1890s was to be overwhelmed by the number of saloons. "There is scarcely a block on any of the poorer avenues which has not its liquor-store, and generally there are two," wrote a visitor to New York in the mid-1890s. "Wherever a street crosses them, there is a saloon on at least one of the corners; sometimes on two, sometimes on three, sometimes, even, on all four. In a stretch of some two miles [along Sixth Avenue] I counted nearly ninety of them." And by 1890 a picture of heavyweight champion John. L. Sullivan hung in nearly every one.

Part of the "sporting life" was garnering attention, and boxers from the beginning drew attention to themselves, spending lavishly and dressing well. "I've got the prettiest clothes you ever saw," John L. Sullivan often bragged. The first black heavyweight champion, Jack Johnson, would buy the fastest cars in the brightest colours. He would gleefully pay speeding tickets by the dozen, peeling off crisp bills from a thick money roll. In one often repeated though most likely apocryphal tale, Jack Johnson was said to be driving his new, bright red roadster through a small town in Georgia. When a local policeman caught sight of a black man behind the wheel of an expensive car, he raced out and stopped him.

"What's the problem, officer?" asked a smiling Johnson.

"Boy, you were driving too fast," said the officer. "And I'm gonna have to fine you fifty dollars."

Johnson, who by now was used to this type of shakedown, reached casually into his pocket and pulled out a roll of hundred-dollar bills. He peeled one off and handed it to the officer.

"What's this?" said the surprised officer. "I can't make change."

"Keep it for now," said Johnson as he started up the car. "I'm coming back this way just as fast as I went through."

* * *

As Dixon's individual star was rising, tales of boxers and their lavish "sporting" lives filled newspapers across the country. First among these was John L. Sullivan. Because the public appetite for news about the heavyweight champion was so great, Sullivan frequently found himself in the papers for his increasingly erratic behaviour.

Late on the evening of March 5, 1890, John L. Sullivan entered Kelly's Saloon on Thirty-first Street in San Francisco. Someone who was there later noted that Sullivan "was maudlin drunk." A dozen or so customers sat in the back, and in one corner, two women and a single man occupied a small table.

From the doorway, Sullivan looked about the saloon, a cigar hanging from his mouth, "his hair dishevelled," and "his battered silk hat ... pushed back on his head." He stumbled from table to table, amusing himself "at the expense of those present." He slapped at one, playfully punched another, offered a "dig in the ribs for the next one and would [then] fall over another," insulting each as he went along. On the whole, the patrons were tolerant, either out of respect for the champion or out of fear.

Sullivan continued on, sometimes "knocking off a hat and pressing his hand over someone's face." Then he sat heavily at an empty table. When he noticed the threesome in the corner, he seemed agitated that they were paying him no attention. So he made "several uncomplimentary remarks," but they ignored him.

Finally, Sullivan stood, knocking over his table, and yelled, "I am John L. Sullivan and I can whip any man in the world!" He then walked over to the trio, and in some demonstration of toughness, he took the cigar from his mouth and "jabbed it into his [own] left eye." He winced and swore. The absurdity of the scene caused many in the room to laugh. But this only further agitated the champion. And when Sullivan regained his focus, he glared at the table of three.

"Do you know who I am?" slurred Sullivan.

"No, I don't know who you are," said the man, "and I don't care."

"Well," said Sullivan, leaning forward and pointing to himself, "I am Sullivan, and I can kill you with one blow."

"I don't care," the man repeated. "And I won't be insulted by anyone."

Sullivan was enraged. The young man stood and let loose a right-hand punch that landed smartly on Sullivan's mouth. The stunned champion staggered back, fell over two chairs, and sprawled on the floor.

Confusion overcame the room.

Realizing what he had done, the young man quickly ran for the door. Sullivan rose to his knees, shaking his head. By the time he got to his feet, Sullivan's friends had entered the saloon and held him back from taking revenge against innocent spectators.

After a time, and likely after a few more drinks, his friends led John L. out of the saloon and safely home.

* * *

On Sunday afternoon, May 5, 1890, the *Lawrence Daily Journal* in Kansas reported that fifty men on horseback rode into the small town of Lexington, South Carolina. Outside the local jail on the main street, they dismounted. Some wore masks, and all were armed. They approached the front door, one carrying a rope, and upon finding the door locked, they knocked it down and entered the jail.

Inside, they found the local sheriff standing by his desk, terrified. The men demanded he give up the cell keys, which he did. The mob then marched down the hall toward the cells, where an eighteen-year-old black man named William Leophart was waiting for trial. Leophart had been arrested for "outraging a white girl."

Leophart watched in horror as the gang tried to unlock his cell door, but they struggled with the key. He was not about to go easily, so he reached through the bars and "seized a club," which he swung wildly at the men. He "fought like a maniac," said one witness, and even managed to injure one of the attackers before the men finally drew their guns and opened fire. "Some 500 shots were poured into the cell," said the same witness. "The man [Leophart] was literally riddled with bullets, which were picked up afterward in the room by the handful."

No one was charged with Leophart's murder.

* * *

Given his epic draw with Cal McCarthy, Dixon began receiving numerous offers to fight. Tom O'Rourke reviewed all with an eye to improving his fighter's purses. One offer that seemed too good to pass on came from the manager of Tommy Kelly, the 105-pound champion, who had been fighting for two weeks in New Jersey's vaudeville theatres. Kelly's manager offered Dixon $250 for one day to fight all comers who could last four rounds. O'Rourke saw this as easy money while he planned for more lucrative fights.

However, when Dixon and O'Rourke arrived at the theatre in New Jersey, they discovered that they had been deceived. Kelly's manager had arranged for three four-round exhibitions for Dixon, all against experienced boxers. O'Rourke was furious. Dixon, though, remained surprisingly calm. Given the cost of travel and the possible loss of face, Dixon thought it wiser to accept the challenge. So on March 1, 1890, Dixon stepped into the ring with Paddy Kearney, and for four rounds, he beat the hapless Kearney senseless. On March 3, Dixon promptly knocked out veteran Joe Ferrell in two rounds. And on March 5, he dropped Jack Carey in three rounds. He then curtly collected his fee and returned to Boston.

* * *

Meantime, Tom O'Rourke arranged for a bout between George Dixon and the English bantamweight champion, Nunc Wallace. O'Rourke believed that winning this fight would solidify Dixon's claim to the title. So in June of 1890, Dixon and O'Rourke set sail for England.

Up to that time, English boxers had long been considered the finest in the world – and for good reason. No American champion had ever defeated an English boxer for a world title. Consequently, expectations ran high that Wallace would easily continue the tradition of victory.

Edward "Nunc" Wallace was born in Birmingham, England, the son of Scottish parents. At twenty-four years of age, he stood five feet two inches tall. He had been a professional fighter for four years and had competed in nineteen bouts, seven with bare knuckles and twelve with gloves. He had only been beaten three times and "those were in gloved competition."

Given the generous publicity, the Dixon-Wallace fight was arranged for the Pelican Club, the famed English gentlemen's club, where patrons wore tuxedos as they watched pugilists fight on a crisp white canvas and sat at a food- and drink-laden table, waited on by gloved servants. The club was filled to capacity that night with those curious to witness the prowess of the upstart challenger.

At 11:00 p.m., on June 27, 1890, George Dixon, weighing 113 pounds, entered the ring at the Pelican Club wearing a red, white, and blue striped robe "with a spread eagle centre, surrounded by two American flags." As Dixon waved and walked casually to his corner where he took a seat on the stool provided, the many Americans in attendance let out a raucous cheer. When one of Dixon's handlers whispered into his ear that the corner had been used by a fighter who had lost earlier in the night, the superstitious Dixon stood and crossed the ring, taking a seat on the opposite side.

Five minutes later, the 112-pound Nunc Wallace entered the room to the enthusiastic applause of the English patrons. He wore a white robe "embroidered with the Prince of Wales plume in black." He stepped through the ropes into the ring, taking a seat in the available corner. After a few minutes of preparation, the boxers rose and removed their robes. Dixon "was nearly naked, wearing a pair of theatrical trunks," while Wallace "wore dark blue drawers."

The referee called the two fighters to the centre of the ring for instructions. They listened, shook hands, and returned to their corners. Meanwhile, the betting began almost immediately, with the odds running at £600 to £400 on Wallace.

From the bell, Wallace was clearly outclassed. He "seemed unable to counter effectively Dixon's terrific blows," reported *The Boston Globe*. And by the third round, he could not land a glancing punch on Dixon without receiving two or three sharp blows in return. To many it seemed Dixon might have ended the fight quickly, but perhaps in the interests of making more money from the betting, Dixon chose instead to spar for points. By the tenth round, as Dixon intensified his assault, Wallace was near to being knocked out and was saved only by the bell.

From table to table in the Pelican Club, the betting shifted quickly, moving two to one and then five to two for Dixon, but "the odds found very few takers." Dixon continued boxing for points, delivering effective combinations from the twelfth through the seventeenth rounds. Then, in the eighteenth round, Dixon "knocked Wallace all over the ring." Clearly, Wallace was incapable of defending himself. He lifted his hands in defeat. "Stop," Wallace was heard to say. "Stop, I'll give in."

A thunderous cheer rose from the crowd at the Pelican Club. The Americans in the crowd raced into the ring where they lifted Dixon onto their shoulders and carried him about the room in riotous celebration. The crowd sang a hearty "For he's a jolly good fellow." Still standing in the ring, Wallace was "badly bruised about the face, and his right eye was cut open." Dixon by contrast showed "no marks of punishment."

Typical of the times, Dixon and O'Rourke remained in England for the remainder of July so that Dixon and Wallace could travel around the country offering boxing fans more than a dozen three-round exhibition bouts.

* * *

Back in Boston, Dixon's victory was a welcome event. "The colored people of the city took great interest in the fight," reported *The Boston Globe*, "and a large number of the prominent colored gentlemen, together with a dozen other sporting men, waited patiently in The Globe sporting rooms last evening for the result of the battle."

On returning to Boston, Dixon and O'Rourke identified the three men standing in the way of Dixon's claim to the featherweight title – Johnny Murphy, who purported to be the featherweight champion of the world; Cal McCarthy, whom Dixon needed to beat to erase any doubts; and Abe Willis, the reigning Australian bantamweight champion. Dixon and O'Rourke knew that a victory over these three would end all doubts about who was the bantamweight and the featherweight champion of the world.

First came the fight with Murphy.

On October 23, 1890, Dixon laced up his gloves to fight Johnny Murphy in a featherweight championship bout in Providence, Rhode Island, for a purse of $1,500 and a side bet of $1,200. "The result of the glove contest between George Dixon and Johnnie Murphy," wrote *The World* of New York, "which takes place at the Gladstone Athletic Club, in Providence, to-night, will be awaited with interest. The New York and Brooklyn sporting fraternity will have his representation at the ring side, and it is assured that the gymnasium of the Club will be taxed to its utmost capacity, for Boston will send a large delegation ... Umpire John Kelly has secured a special parlor car, which will be attached to the Shore Line train leaving the Grand Central Depot at 1 o'clock to-day. This car will be side-tracked at Providence, and leaves that city at midnight if the decision is given at that time. The Stonington line boat last night carried more than a hundred admirers of boxing to Providence."

Johnny Murphy, muscular and with a square head and close-cropped hair, hailed from England but had moved to America as a child. He now called Boston home. He had been fighting for six years and claimed to be the 114-pound featherweight champion. Although his self-styled championship was more bravado than reality, he was certainly a formidable opponent. And both O'Rourke and Dixon were happy to sell the fight as a championship bout.

Dixon and Murphy both entered the ring that night at 9:35. The crowd, more favourable to Murphy, jeered at Dixon, calling out insults and threats. Dixon ignored them as he listened to the instructions from the referee. The fighters shook hands and the bell sounded.

From the start, the fight belonged to Dixon. He moved with speed and grace, anticipating every effort by Murphy and responding with devastating effect. He threw well-designed combinations to Murphy's body and sharp uppercuts and overhands to his head.

Murphy, a determined fighter, remained standing. For fourteen rounds, as the crowed taunted Dixon, Murphy held up under the rain of blows. After a time, Murphy appeared dazed and ready to fall. But Dixon refused to finish his opponent.

In the fifteenth round, Murphy's cornermen claimed that Dixon had thrown a low blow, but the referee waved the claim off and let the fight continue. The crowd howled in protest. Thereafter, perhaps remembering the Wright bout, Dixon seemed more cautious, afraid of losing on a foul. Murphy took advantage of Dixon's caution and pressed for an advantage. Even still, Murphy could not land a solid punch. Round after round, Dixon kept dodging and dancing, and countering with decisive blows.

A contemporary drawing of the fight shows Murphy and Dixon in a tight clinch, as they fall heavily to a ring floor of broad wooden planks surrounded by ropes. Over them stands a referee with wide sideburns and wearing a long coat. Sitting ringside are men dressed in top hats and long coats, while further back, the poorer patrons perch on wooden boxes.

In round thirty-seven, Dixon rushed Murphy into the corner and threw a right and left to his head. Murphy slumped but did not fall. He lifted his hands and weathered more blows from Dixon before slipping under a right hand and staggering to the opposite side of the ring. Dixon followed and delivered another sharp strike to the head that dropped Murphy to his knees. As Dixon hovered, his hand cocked back, Murphy pulled himself up by the ropes. Once Murphy stood free, Dixon let loose a furious combination that might well have finished Murphy had the bell not rung.

Murphy rallied in the next round, pressing Dixon, who now dodged what Murphy offered and responded with efficient counterblows. But Murphy began to fade. In the fortieth round, almost two hours after the fight began, Murphy could take no more. Enduring one more Dixon combination, Murphy collapsed into the arms of his trainers, and the fight was called. Those in attendance could not help but notice that Dixon hardly seemed fatigued.

The crowd shouted their disgust.

"When he fought Johnny Murphy and beat him in forty rounds," observed Nat Fleischer, "Dixon had to do all his fighting in the center of the ring, so maneuvering his man as not to get near the ropes where the thugs could hit his legs with their black jacks and slug shots." Yet Dixon maintained an exceptional discipline. He rarely showed anger at the constant abuse, and he always projected a positive, agreeable face to the public.

Still, the constant racist reproach from white fans must have taken its toll.

* * *

In July 1890, the *Daily Tribune* of Salt Lake City ran a long article about the growing interest in the bantamweight and featherweight classes of boxing. The headline series, common to the age, ran: "Little Giants of the Ring. The Bantams and Feather-Weights Crowding the Big Fellows. A Swarm of Lilliputian Fighters. The Product of the Boxing Schools – More Scientific, Pluckier and Cleverer Than the Heavy-Weights – Some Interesting Examples – Great Matches Among the Little Men."

"Since the Kilrain-Sullivan fight," read the article, "no event in the prize ring has been regarded with livelier interest than the battle for the bantam-weight championship of the world between George Dixon and Nunc Wallace." The comparison to John L. was clear.

"That the triumphant tour of John L. Sullivan should have been emulated by a bantam is sufficiently amusing to those who have not been observant of the tendencies of the ring, but to the insiders, it is full of significance. The day of the 'little un' has come. In numbers and superior science, he is crowding the big fellows to the wall. He is chock full of grit and would rather be killed than suffer defeat. His little body sometimes contains the heart of a lion. It is not surprising that the big fellows should hold him in such high esteem, looking at him admiringly and wonder at the concentrated lightning style in which he sets to work on an opponent."

Around this time, Dixon began a habit of celebrating his victories with a drink. After a fight, Dixon and O'Rourke would make their way to the local saloon, where O'Rourke would have a few glasses of beer, while Dixon, noted the New York *Sun* not long after his death, "would get a pocketful of money and start opening wine and buying drinks for everyone like a millionaire out on a lark. The colored fighter had a big heart and slipped many a five or ten spot to broken down boxers and old friends. Outside of the ring, Dixon was a very quiet man. He never talked fight of his own will and never got into a row if he could help it."

At the very threshold of his greatest success, Dixon's concurrent embrace of the sporting life would bring his greatest failure.

Round Five

Left Hand Body Blow: *[In] a left hand body blow ... the head is thrown slightly to the right and your opponent's left arm will pass over your shoulder. As quickly as possible lead with your left for the body. If the blow lands it is usually a very telling one as your opponent is coming toward you, while the weight of your body is also flowing towards him. This same blow may be delivered at the face but it is not so effective as when landed on the body from the same position. This is one of the best as well as one of the most difficult blows I know of. When landing a left hand blow on the body, always try to hit squarely in the pit of the stomach as it is the part of the body which most affects the wind. Be careful not to stoop too low or put your head too far forward as your opponent may land a blow by swinging his right arm around behind the back. I will explain this 'behind the back' blow I refer to later. In slipping away from a left hand blow at the face always try and get your head just beyond your opponent's elbow.*

— George Dixon, "A Lesson in Boxing" (1893)

Throughout the nineteenth century, both bare-knuckled fighting and gloved boxing were popular pastimes among the poor and working class. Their participation in boxing naturally followed, and often reflected, the economic, social, and ethnic divisions and conflicts within the neighbourhoods of large cities. And it was no coincidence that boxing grew in popularity at the same time of growing labour strikes, gang warfare, and racial strife. It was also no coincidence that the ranks of boxers often filled with people who felt the most social and economic pressure.

America's first "immigrants," the Irish, dominated early boxing as did black Americans. In the late nineteenth and early twentieth centuries, the growth of Italian and Jewish immigration saw the inclusion of these groups in boxing. In fact, during these early years, fighters routinely identified themselves by their ethnicity as a means to cultivate support. "Irish" Eddie Finnegan, Abe "The Little Hebrew" Attell, and George "Little Chocolate" Dixon are all examples. The ethnic nickname was not always derogatory. Rather, it was a means to provide group identification with a particular fighter.

* * *

As George Dixon's reputation grew, he received more attention as the presumed bantamweight champion. Naturally, Cal McCarthy, who still claimed the American bantamweight championship, took exception. In November of 1890, while Dixon sparred at a vaudeville performance in New York City with Ben Williams, the impresario of the evening, Tom Ward, introduced George Dixon to the audience as the "Bantamweight Champion of the World." As it turned out – and one imagines by Tom O'Rourke's design – Cal McCarthy was also present. While Dixon was receiving applause from the audience, McCarthy sauntered onto the stage and addressed the audience.

"Ladies and gentlemen," he said, "George Dixon is not the bantamweight champion of the world and will not be until he has defeated me. I have won the title and am willing to uphold it against Dixon or any other man. I have never been defeated, and until then the bantam championship is mine."

The wily Ward did not miss a beat. "In the absence of Tom O'Rourke, George Dixon's manager and backer, I am authorized to look after Dixon's interests. I will match Dixon against McCarthy for any amount of money that he can put up. Dixon is the bantamweight champion of the world and won the title in this country and England. Mr. O'Rourke will be in town tomorrow and he will be ready to match against McCarthy."

Dixon was either genuinely taken aback, or he feigned indignation. Afterward he spoke with a reporter from *The Boston Globe*. "I was surprised at McCarthy's behavior," Dixon said. "I met him in the bar next to the theatre before I went to the stage. We shook hands and drank together and talked for a few minutes upon general topics. I excused myself and went to dress. The next I saw of him was when he came upon the stage. I don't think it was a square deal. It is his own fault that he did not fight me again. He said that he was not satisfied and the money was promptly put up. He failed to agree on the grounds that his arm was injured. He has made a lot of talking. For while I never defeated a champion, I have stopped and put out several men that he could only make draws with. I will meet him and fight him for going around talking about his lost chances."

Despite Dixon's apparent upset at McCarthy's behaviour, it seems clear that he and O'Rourke were becoming effective at promoting a good fight for a good purse.

The press took interest in the fight and in the growing reputation of George Dixon. *The Boston Globe* provided an almost daily report on Dixon's coming fights and his life. On February 5, 1891, the *Globe* gave its readers a brief promotion of Dixon the boxer. "[He] is a born fighter," the article read. "He never received a lesson in boxing in his life, and what he knows about the art, he picked up himself. His career in the ring has been remarkable, and but for an unjust decision, he would have a clear record. No colored pugilist has ever gained as many honors in the ring as has Dixon, and in fact, there are but few white men that can boast of a better or equal the doughty colored lad's record. He has also done the one thing that only one other American has succeeded in doing, won a battle in England.

"Despite his great reputation, Dixon is one of the most modest and unassuming men that ever stepped into the ring. Unlike most men of his calling, he has never become inflated over his successes, and he is just the same today as he was three years ago when he had but little reputation. Unless interviewed, he never talks fight, and he has been known to sit for two hours listening to arguments about fights and fighters without speaking a word. He also stands today as one of the finest development men in the country, and a number of prominent men who are interested in physical culture have been examining him daily at the gymnasium, where he has been training. He has surprised them all by his remarkable 'build,' and they all state that it is on only one man of a thousand that the serratus magnus muscles stand out as prominently as they do on Dixon."

Dixon's popularity was unusual in that it blurred racial lines. Few black public figures to that date had ever been so well received by the broader population.

As with John L. Sullivan, it seemed the sports-minded public in the early 1890s had an insatiable appetite for Dixon. Later that same February, *The Boston Globe* offered its readers additional insights into his training.

"About four to five weeks before his fight, Dixon begins to train. The first day he is given a physic, and for the next three days he does nothing except take short walks without sweating. During the remainder of the week, he does light work. The next week his walk is increased and is kept increasing until a couple of days before the battle, when he takes only short walks and punches the ball. Every morning he rises at 7, dresses himself in his sweaters and takes a 15 minute stroll about the streets. On his return he eats an orange and 10 minutes later has his breakfast, which generally consists of rolled oats, as many soft-boiled eggs as he feels disposed to eat, bread and butter and a cup of weak tea. He then takes a rest until 9 o'clock, when he starts out with his companion to do his roadwork. He goes off at an ordinary walk and increases it till he has travelled five miles. Then he starts to return, and during his journey back runs or walks, as he feels inclined.

"On his arrival at the gymnasium, an attendant strips him and rubs him down thoroughly with Turkish towels. He then takes a shower bath of lukewarm water, after which he is again rubbed down and taken to this room. There he receives a hand-rubbing with a preparation of liniment until he is dry. He then dresses himself in dry clothing and goes to his manager's home, where he eats dinner at 1 o'clock. Sometimes it consists of roast beef, lamb, steaks, fresh fish, potatoes, stewed tomatoes, a little pudding and tea. After the meal, he rests until 3 o'clock, when he again visits the gymnasium to take his afternoon exercise. After punching the light ball 20 minutes, he uses the half pound dumbbell and Indian clubs for the next 20 minutes, and the last 20 minutes he runs around the track. He then goes through the same process of rubbing as he does in the morning. At 6 o'clock he eats his supper, which usually consists of eggs or steak, whichever he prefers. At 9 o'clock he goes to bed, and sleeps as peacefully as if nothing was on his mind."

* * *

The rematch with Cal McCarthy was set for February 5, 1891. Some three thousand people arrived before 8:00 p.m. to watch the bout at the newly built amphitheatre called the Puritan Athletic Club. Excitement ran high for what had become a grudge match. But owners of the rival Jefferson Club went to court earlier that day to stop the match, believing they had the contract to offer the fight. The judge issued the stay, but no one told the crowd waiting outside the Puritan. Tempers flared. Many of the fans outside, "shivering in the keen westerly wind which whistled through Borden Avenue," began to "pound and kick the doors." Not long afterward, police arrived and dispersed the now angry mob, while management spoke to the fighters' backers.

"I have been instructed by the management," said a representative of the Puritan Club to Dixon's and McCarthy's seconds, "to say that this contest will not take place here tonight on account of legal difficulties. It is not the fault of the management. The directors have done everything in their power to bring this contest off to your satisfaction."

Back in Boston the next day, Dixon and O'Rourke were angry. "McCarthy is not anxious to fight," said an agitated Dixon, "and he showed it very plainly. He is talking about fighting with me with only skin gloves, but there is no money in such a battle. If there was, I would readily consent to go at him at that kind of fighting, and I am sure I can whip him with skin gloves as with four or five ounce gloves. It's the 'stuff' [money] I'm after, and had the fight come off Thursday night I would have had lots of it in my pockets this morning."

When asked about the chances of the rematch happening, Dixon responded, "There are some sporting men in New York who think they can have matters arranged so that we can meet in New Jersey in a week or so, and they are to let us know this afternoon if the battle can be decided without interference in that State. If this match falls through, I am going to take a rest for a year, for I have trained hard four times within the past year, and that is enough to weaken anyone."

Dixon also directed his anger at the Puritan Club. "The managers of the Puritan Club have not given us anything for our trouble," said Dixon, "and when O'Rourke spoke to them about the matter, they did not seem inclined to give up, although we were guaranteed a certain amount when we signed the articles."

On February 9, 1891, the Puritan Club officially declared the match off. Both parties withdrew their stakes. Over the next few days, the intensity of the anger increased. McCarthy publicly complained that Dixon was unwilling to meet him because of a disagreement over glove size. The next day, O'Rourke snapped back.

"Oh! That fellow is trying to make people believe he is the only one that wants to fight," said O'Rourke, "but we are satisfied that he is looking for a hole to crawl out of in making a new match. When he talks of fighting for a stake with skin gloves, he knows well there is no money for a fighter in such a battle. If some good club will offer a reasonable purse, we will put up as much stake money as McCarthy can raise. The gloves are immaterial, for George will fight him with the smallest-sized hand coverings the club will allow."

No doubt the public dispute increased interest in the fight. Within days a new venue was found and a new date was set – February 20, 1891. The Hudson River Athletic Club of Jersey City put up a purse of $4,000. McCarthy quickly accepted and suggested a side bet of $2,000. Not long afterward, the date was changed again, to February 27, only to be cancelled a few days later when the city shut down the fight.

Dixon was training on the speed bag when he heard the news. He was visibly disappointed. "It will be a long time before they get me to train again for a fight in that section of New York," he told reporters. "They have fooled me twice, and then they do not half pay me for my trouble in getting fit. I have not signed articles with this club, and now I suppose they will not give me a cent to pay for my week's training."

Meantime, O'Rourke authorized a California club to approve a fight between George Dixon and Abe Willis, the champion bantamweight of Australia, to be set in San Francisco sometime between April and June, 1891. On the following morning, an offer was received from Troy, New York, to host the Dixon-McCarthy fight. The articles were signed on March 6 and the fight was on again.

On the morning before his March 31, 1891, rematch with Cal McCarthy in Troy, New York, George was busy training, taking his morning run along Beacon Street in Boston, when a man working on a paving crew saw him coming along the sidewalk and stepped in front of him. "Hey," the workman said, "you training for a six days' race or something?"

Dixon stopped and shook his head. "Look," he said, "just mind your own business." He turned and started across the street.

The workman was enraged. He bent down and picked up a piece of paving stone and hurled the stone at Dixon's head. Dixon saw the movement from the corner of his eye, and his reaction was quick. He ducked and turned toward the man. The workman's mates, perhaps recognizing Dixon, quickly grabbed the offending worker by the arms and asked why he had done that. But the man just pulled away, saying nothing. Dixon would later make a complaint to the police and a warrant was issued for the man's arrest.

Later that evening, George Dixon and Tom O'Rourke boarded an overnight train for Troy, New York.

Cal McCarthy and his retinue arrived in Troy before dawn, having taken a Citizens' Line steamboat from New York City up the Hudson River. After gathering their bags at the dock, the group made their way to The Troy House Hotel in town. There, McCarthy took a bath, ate breakfast, and then took a nap. At 10:00 a.m., he woke and, fearing that he might be carrying an extra pound or so, made his way to a Turkish bath to sweat away the excess weight. When he arrived at the bath he weighed himself only to discover that he was an even 115 pounds. So he returned to the hotel and fell sleep until 2:30. After he woke, he dressed and walked with his trainers to a saloon on River Street, where he and Dixon had agreed to be officially weighed.

"Where's Dixon?" McCarthy asked as he entered the saloon and approached the scales.

"He'll be here in a minute," a man at the scales said.

At that moment, Dixon entered the saloon with Tom O'Rourke.

"Hello, Cal," said Dixon, smiling. When he reached the scales, he shook McCarthy's hand. "You look pretty well."

McCarthy smiled and looked Dixon over. "I'm feeling tip-top, thank you," he said. "I don't know that I have any the best of you."

From behind Dixon, a stern-faced O'Rourke looked McCarthy over and then tapped Dixon on the shoulder and nodded. It was time to get down to business. Both men understood. They stripped to the waist and stood next to the scales. The judge of the scales, "Handsome" Billy Madden, fixed the scales at 115 pounds. McCarthy stepped on first. The brass beam did not move. He smiled. "See what your exact weight is, Cal," said someone in the group. Madden moved the indicator until the scale tipped at 114½ pounds.

Then Dixon stepped on the scale. As with McCarthy, the scale did not move. But Dixon did not stay on the scale for an exact weight. They dressed as the fight referee arrived and removed three sets of four-ounce gloves from an alligator bandbox. Both fighters and their seconds inspected the gloves and gave their approval. Then, when the weigh-in was complete, the two left the saloon, each making his way to separate restaurants to eat. Dixon had a porterhouse steak, while McCarthy had a double portion of lamb chops, three poached eggs, and tea.

Afterward, both retired to their rooms and slept until they were awakened for the fight.

* * *

At 7:00 p.m., several hundred men stood outside a large, wooden building on the outskirts of Troy, New York. Normally used as bicycle track, the building had been converted into a temporary boxing venue to accommodate the unusually large crowd expected for the anticipated rematch. As the doors opened, allowing the crowd to enter, people streamed down Federal Street toward the building. *The Boston Globe* noted, "Some of them wore diamonds, and some did not, but those who didn't have sparklers appeared to be just as anxious to see the contest as were the others."

The demand for Dixon-McCarthy tickets was so great that counterfeit tickets were being sold at five dollars apiece. The doorkeepers did not discover the fraud until close to two hundred false-ticket holders had entered. By the time of the fight, more than two thousand people were seated and standing in close company, waiting for the bout to begin.

At 8:00 p.m., a delegation of local politicians filed in, smoking cigars and laughing. They walked slowly to their well-placed reserved seats near the ring. The ring itself was well laid out under excellent lighting with good ventilation. The ring posts, noted the *Globe* reporter, were "heavily padded with cotton covered with red muslin."

At 9:37 p.m., George Dixon appeared in the hall with Tom O'Rourke just behind him. A wild cheer rose up from the crowd. The men made their way, slowly, through the crowd to the ring.

The betting had long since commenced, with the action heavy and most leaning toward Dixon. At the same time, Cal McCarthy had also entered the room, earning similar cheers from the crowd. Both fighters slipped through the ropes at about 10:15 p.m. and found their stools in opposite corners.

For nearly a minute more, the assembled crowd offered raucous cheers and thunderous applause. At the referee's instruction, both fighters stood and removed their robes. Dixon wore white trunks. Murphy was in blue. The cornermen put gloves on the combatants, carefully lacing and firmly tying them at the wrist. Time was called at 10:25 p.m., and the two men met in the centre of the ring where referee Jerry Dunn explained the rules.

Dixon and McCarthy shook hands and returned to their corners.

When the bell rang, McCarthy wasted no time, striking first with a left-hand blow to Dixon's neck. Dixon countered with a left to McCarthy's eye. The crowd roared approval with each blow. McCarthy again delivered a left to Dixon's neck and the two clinched. When they broke, McCarthy threw another left to Dixon's eye and then ducked Dixon's "deadly right." McCarthy countered the missed punch with a sharp cut to Dixon's jaw and yet another to his neck. As the bell rang, the betting in the room moved quickly toward McCarthy.

In the second round, Dixon was quick with his left and caught McCarthy in the ribs. McCarthy countered but missed his target. Dixon smiled. McCarthy lunged with a roundhouse left, and again, he missed. Dixon returned with a right to McCarthy's stomach and added a quick right-left combination to the head. McCarthy clinched to save himself. But Dixon pushed him off and delivered a stinging right to the jaw that left McCarthy "sprawling in the rosin." He stood quickly, shaking his head, while the referee checked him over. Then, when the referee stepped away, Dixon made a rush to finish McCarthy off.

But the bell rang to end the round.

In the third, Dixon picked up where he had left off. He delivered a left to McCarthy's ear and then sidestepped the response. Dixon returned with two more shots, but McCarthy "took his medicine gamely" and the fight ebbed back toward him.

In the fourth and fifth rounds, McCarthy proved adept at slipping punches and applying evasive tactics to stay in the fight. In the sixth, he surprised Dixon with a solid shot to the chin. But Dixon stayed focused and countered with a devastating combination to McCarthy's head and ribs. In the seventh, McCarthy took to circling the ring while Dixon tried to pin him into the corner, where he delivered hard rights to the jaw.

In the eighth round, perhaps weary from the intensity, the fighters stopped moving about the ring and stood in the centre exchanging heavy blows. Dixon bloodied McCarthy's nose, while McCarthy drew blood from Dixon's mouth. By the tenth, McCarthy showed a second wind, offering fine punches, but few effectively connected. Dixon returned with a thunderous right to McCarthy's jaw, leaving McCarthy staggering backward until he cleared his head and delivered a surprising counterpunch to Dixon's jaw. The punch clearly registered as McCarthy managed three more blows without Dixon's response. In the eleventh, McCarthy took the initiative, catching Dixon again and again with rights and lefts. McCarthy's cornermen roared their approval, while Dixon's assistants registered their concern.

At the start of the twelfth round, McCarthy pressed on, striking Dixon with a solid right to the chin. Dixon held his ground and took back the initiative by moving in close and pounding on McCarthy "unmercifully." When McCarthy tried to clinch, Dixon kept the short jabs flying until the bell. In the thirteenth round, the two fighters seemed content to rest, circling and offering few exchanges.

In the fourteenth, McCarthy returned with energy and delivered a stinging shot to Dixon's chin. Dixon replied with set combinations to McCarthy's chest. In the fifteenth, Dixon threw a hard left that missed and opened him up to a devastating combination by McCarthy. Dixon's knees buckled and he appeared "groggy." McCarthy pressed his advantage until the bell.

In the sixteenth and seventeenth rounds, McCarthy delivered more blows to Dixon's bleeding mouth. But in the eighteenth, Dixon responded by hitting McCarthy sharply on the nose with a left. He rushed forward and caught McCarthy twice more in the head until McCarthy clinched. In the nineteenth through twenty-first rounds, Dixon regained a decisive edge, pressing and punching, punishing McCarthy, who seemed unable to find an effective response.

Finally, in the twenty-second round, McCarthy came off his stool on wobbly legs. It was quickly clear to all that he was avoiding Dixon until he felt his strength return. But Dixon did not hesitate to strike. He "went at his man like an enraged lion liberated from his cage." He delivered a devastating combination – a hard right, then a quick left – to McCarthy's head. McCarthy was stunned and he staggered. Dixon allowed McCarthy a moment to steady himself then rushed in with a hard left, sending McCarthy to the canvas.

McCarthy rose, slowly. He looked with defeated eyes at his corner, but his seconds encouraged him on. So McCarthy stood and moved toward Dixon, hoping perhaps to clinch. But Dixon would have none of it. He delivered another stunning left that again floored McCarthy. This time the referee stood over the prone fighter and counted to seven before McCarthy rose. Once on his feet, McCarthy managed to hug Dixon, who kept delivering shots to McCarthy's ribs. For a third time, McCarthy fell to the canvas, exhausted.

One of McCarthy's cornermen sprayed his man with water, and McCarthy revived enough to crawl to the post. Dixon started back to his corner. But when he turned and saw McCarthy back on his feet, he rushed at him, striking with his left. McCarthy fell leaden into the corner. This time McCarthy's seconds found a towel and flung it into the ring. Referee Dunn picked it up and turned to the crowd. "McCarthy quits," he shouted. "Dixon is the winner and new world champion."

What followed was a "perfect storm of applause" as both exhausted fighters were carried on the shoulders of their supporters to their respective dressing rooms.

McCarthy had tears streaming down his cheeks.

* * *

After his victory and the circus that followed the McCarthy fight, George Dixon laid low for a few months. Likely, he spent time at home with Kitty and out on the town in Boston. Although he was mentioned in newspapers across the country almost every day, most of the reporting was in anticipation of a championship fight with Abe Willis, the bantamweight champion of Australia.

As training for the Willis bout, Dixon took a fight with Martin Flaherty in Chicago. Flaherty was from Lowell, Massachusetts, and in five fights, he was undefeated. Flat-nosed with thick shoulders, Flaherty had made a name for himself as a brawler. While Dixon was the recognized champion of the world, the crowd in Chicago was clearly hostile. As the fight began, Dixon realized he could easily dispatch Flaherty, but the local police, concerned about the mob reaction, asked Dixon to hold back for five rounds. Only in the sixth round was Dixon finally allowed to "cut loose." At that point, Dixon began pummelling Flaherty. Flaherty clinched, and in the tussle, he raised his head sharply and cut Dixon, who began to bleed heavily.

Dixon was furious.

He backed Flaherty into his corner with devastating combinations until the police finally stepped in to stop the fight. The crowd was enraged and made clear their anger at Dixon. Concerned for his safety, Dixon did not stay long. In fact, he and O'Rourke immediately took a train from Chicago to California, where Dixon was scheduled to face Abe Willis.

* * *

The fight with Abe Willis in California was cast as the "first fight for the world's championship in this country." The July 27 edition of *The Boston Globe* noted "the amount of money offered [for this fight] is also the largest that has been offered in this country for men in this class." To drum up more interest, the paper also said that Willis was considered a great fighter, whose "reputation was heralded throughout his country long before he reached these shores." Indeed, "he did not confine himself to fighting men in his own class, but he met several good featherweights."

Abe Willis was born in Woolahra, not far from Sydney, Australia, on June 15, 1868. Like Dixon, he stood five feet three. He was said to have quick hands and a tenacious presence in the ring. He began boxing in 1884 as a bare-knuckled fighter, defeating his first opponent in three and a half hours. In nearly a dozen fights afterward, Willis was said to have lost only three, two to Australian featherweight "Rocks" Griffo and once to Billy Murphy who was, at the time, more than ten pounds heavier.

The wily O'Rourke knew that a victory over Abe Willis would ensure both the bantamweight championship of the world and even bigger purses. He had been so intent on this fight coming to pass that he was prepared to travel with Dixon to Australia to meet Willis. However, the clubs in Australia would not offer enough money to make the venture worthwhile, so Willis sailed to San Francisco and made arrangements for the fight. O'Rourke had said to the interested clubs that it would take an unprecedented $5,000 to the winner and $500 expenses for the fight to happen. The California Athletic Club in San Francisco at first refused, but the demand to see the fight was so great that the club finally relented.

Waiting for the fight to be arranged, Willis gave an exhibition bout in San Francisco. His "showing, on that occasion, did not impress the sports very favorably, but it satisfied the club," said *The Boston Globe*. "[Willis] is a good infighter, but from good authorities, it is learned that he does not know how to use his left. In other words, he is nothing more than a right-handed fighter. He is also said to have a bad habit of turning his head around just before he swings his right."

No doubt George Dixon took careful notes.

The racism of the California Athletic Club was more than obvious in their less than flattering assessment of Dixon as he, like Willis, demonstrated his skills in an exhibition bout in San Francisco prior to the big fight. "The Californians looked him over very carefully, and the majority of them felt as if they would like to express to Dixon their sorrow for him coming so far to get a 'licking.'"

The spectators were certain that Willis would make "a chopping block" of him. They also said Dixon was "more of a jockey than a fighter." It is possible that Dixon was holding back, helping the betting odds work in his favour. But it also seems clear that the local sports were colour blind to Dixon's obvious talents. Few had seen him fight before, and fewer still knew of his relentless and impressive improvement in style and form with each bout.

For the fight, Dixon had little difficulty keeping his weight at 114½ pounds, while Willis, it was said, was "having a hard time getting the weight [he had gained since his arrival] off." Dixon took to training at a local gym called Neptune Gardens in Alameda, five miles from the city. Willis trained at Sausalito.

A Baltimore newspaper, *The Morning Herald*, described Dixon's training on July 19. "George Dixon, champion bantamweight of America, is considered by all who have visited him at his quarters, the best self-trained man that ever stepped into fighting shoes," noted the *Herald* reporter in San Francisco. "Tom O'Rourke is ever present, but there is little need of his services. Dixon has several new ideas in training, which will probably be adopted by other pugilists in this city. Although always confident of winning, Dixon never goes into training with the idea of doing up an opponent in two or three rounds. He always prepares himself for a long battle. He is doing so now. Bantams as a rule fight longer than heavyweights. In keeping their arms before them for 40 or 50 rounds the muscles become strained and then cramped.

"Dixon's methods are to overcome this. His plan is simple. He uses a small pair of dumb-bells, and with one in either hand he faces an imaginary opponent. As he feints, leads and ducks before the 'spook' enemy, he advances on one and then the other foot. The weight of the dumb-bells strengthens his arms without binding the muscles.

"Besides running regularly on the rounds, Dixon does considerable leg work in the Neptune Gardens building. Standing on the same spot he gets his legs in a running motion and covers what would be five miles in ordinary running. He times himself by the number of minutes it would take him to cover that distance. He never moves off the spot, however, but swings his arms, throws out his chest and goes through the movements of running without making headway."

As the interest in the Dixon-Willis fight grew, so too did the odds and the betting. Making the interest even greater were rumours suggesting another venue, the Occidental Club, was likely to take the match from the California Athletic Club. A local bookmaker named Phil Archibald, originally from Australia, had "a large sized bone to pick with the California Club." It was said that he had long been a backer of the Australians "ever since he left Kangerooland." In counterbalance, Tom O'Rourke, who was a friend of the Occidental Club's treasurer and was offered $400 to move the fight there, defended the present site for the bout. In the end, Willis finally said he would abide by the agreement and fight at the California Club.

On the morning of July 27, Abe Willis took a long run over the mountains of Marin County, and after being rubbed down at Ryan's Hotel in Sausalito, he weighed in at 113 pounds. George Dixon continued to work out at Neptune Gardens in Alameda. Said one reporter of Dixon, he "looks as quick as a bullet and as healthy as a prize pig at a State fair, although not quite as beefy." At the California Club the seating was arranged and set, and the betting on the fight was now $80 to $100 for Willis.

* * *

On July 28, 1891, the long-awaited Bantamweight Championship of the World took place at the California Club. The final purse was set for $5,000, the largest ever offered for a bantamweight fight, with $750 going to the loser. Both fighters were in excellent shape as they made their way to the club. Dixon travelled to the bout across the bay from Neptune Gardens, "feeling excellent and looking fine," while Willis arrived from Sausalito early and went right to the California Club.

Said one reporter, Willis looked in "splendid" condition. When asked for his thoughts by a *Boston Globe* reporter, Willis said, "I know I've got a hard man to whip, but I feel as confident of doing it has I have in my past fights. Win or lose my friends can rest assured that I will make the best fight I can, and they will have no fault to find with me. I feel as strong as an ox, and think I can fight all night if necessary."

The fighters weighed in at the club at 3:00 p.m. Willis tipped the scales at 114½ pounds, while Dixon weighed in at 115. The referee was a veteran of the ring, a gentleman named Hiram Cook. The betting, which had commenced long before the fight, was now unusually heavy, with bookmakers active throughout the day and into the evening. The initial interest in Willis now moved toward Dixon as word of his fights on the east coast began to spread west. Odds of ten to eight in favour of Dixon were easily covered. Tom O'Rourke arrived at the club and quickly found Phil Archibald, Willis's backer. Archibald wanted to lay a side bet of $2,500 on Willis. O'Rourke, smiling at Archibald, happily accepted.

By 7:00 p.m., a "big, noisy crowd" had already gathered at the club. Prices for tickets had been lowered so that "a portion of the tough element" could enter and watch. A preliminary fight was offered, but it was a weak showing and only made the anticipation for the main event even greater. At 8:30 p.m., Dixon and Willis finally entered. As they met in the centre of the ring where the referee explained the rules, the two looked like "pygmy giants, with hair cropped so closely that they were white-headed." The two shook hands and smiled, while the patrons went as "quiet as church mice."

The sharp clang of the bell broke the silence, and the two fighters sprang up from their corners and approached. Dixon showed himself to be cautious at first. He feigned two blows to draw Willis out. Willis responded twice. Then Dixon unloaded a fierce right to Willis's jaw, dropping Willis to the canvas. The crowd jeered. Though stunned, Willis was quick to his feet, shaking his head and then rushing at Dixon. The two exchanged furious blows until the bell rang.

In round two, the fighters stood toe to toe. Dixon allowed this even though in-close fighting was Willis's strength. The two clinched, broke, and clinched again. When they broke the second time, Dixon committed himself to a left-hand "half-arm swing" to Willis's ribs. Willis countered with two sharp rights to Dixon's face. Dixon just smiled and said, "That's the way."

Frustrated, Willis threw more blows to little effect.

In round three, Dixon stepped up his assault, delivering "straight drives from the shoulder, swings, and uppercuts as plentiful as checks in the Chinese quarters." Willis tried to respond with solid rights to Dixon's head, but Dixon ducked each punch. Leaning forward, Dixon then delivered a "crusher" to Willis's jaw. Willis was notably rattled but kept on swinging.

Dixon continued to have the upper hand in round four, using his left hand to devastating effect, landing nearly every punch he threw. Willis, meanwhile, tried to find an opening for his right, but Dixon had studied his opponent well.

He left no holes.

Dixon racked up more points, delivering two forceful lefts to Willis's jaw. Willis reeled. Dixon stepped in close for "10 or 15 seconds of infighting, buzz-saw fashion." And by the bell, the punishment on Willis had taken its toll.

By round five, it was clear the day belonged to Dixon. He opened the round with a "hard shot" left to Willis's neck and another left to the ribs. Willis was "dazed." Dixon moved to alternate hand combinations to the ribs and then to the stomach. He used a fast right that caught Willis on the nose and followed with a left-hand uppercut to the stomach. Willis was winded and he doubled up. Finally, Willis fell "helpless" to the ropes. He shook off the assault, and then staggered back to the centre of the ring, where he met another left hand to the chest. Willis dropped to a knee, but rose again, only to receive a final left to the jaw. He fell unconscious to the canvas, moving only once before the count of ten was made and the fight was called for George Dixon.

As had been the case after the Cal McCarthy fight, a large crowd of "colored men" gathered in front of *The Boston Globe* building, waiting to hear the news. When it came, they cheered wildly then "rushed in different directions to tell the rest of the population the good news."

* * *

At the same time that George Dixon was defeating Abe Willis, John L. Sullivan was in Chicago, touring with his vaudeville group. As an effort to combat his drinking, he was taking a daily injection of bi-chloride of gold. "He will be under the same restrictions as other patients of Dr. Lester C. Keeley," reported *The Boston Globe*, "and his disease – for it has been proved that drunkenness is a disease – it is expected will gracefully yield to the gentle influences exerted by Dr. Keeley's inspiring cure."

Said Sullivan about the process, "The doc says drunkenness is a disease. That hits me between the eyes, and I wouldn't mind giving his treatment a crack." The next day it was reported that Sullivan left for southern California "in a state of helpless drunkenness." He had been in a fight that night and was knocked down, drawing blood from his nose. "Sullivan was drunk nearly all last week," read the news report, "but managed to sober up every night for the theatrical performance."

* * *

Having beaten the American bantamweight champion Cal McCarthy, the British bantamweight champion Nunc Wallace, the Australian bantamweight champion Abe Willis, and the leading bantamweight challenger Johnny Murphy, George Dixon could now lay uncontested claim to the Bantamweight Championship of the World. He had officially become the first black champion in boxing.

Yet he wanted more.

He now set his sights on another title, the Featherweight Championship of the World.

Round Six

Cross Counter Blow: *The cross counter blow is often called 'give and take.' It derives the name of 'give and take' from one man allowing his opponent an opportunity to land a blow in order to return a more effective one. Cut No. 5 illustrates my opponent landing his left hand upon my jaw, while my right hand has also landed upon his jaw. In order to land my right hand upon his jaw, I was compelled to leave an opening, which he took advantage of with his left hand, consequently I take to give. My object is to land a quicker and more effective blow than he. The blow which lands first in an exchange of this kind will break the force of the other man's blow as it stops the weight of the body coming towards him. Always bear in mind that it is not necessary to swing with your right hand in order to land an effective cross counter blow. The straight blow, in fact, is much the better, as it is delivered from the shoulder and usually brings better results.*
  – George Dixon, "A Lesson in Boxing" (1893)

1892 was the single most murderous year of lynching in America. Over a period of twelve months, more than 160 black Americans were lawlessly hanged, while countless others were shot or tortured to death. And though this reign of terror was pervasive throughout all of America in 1892, it remained most rabid and most dangerous in the American South.

1892 was also the year George Dixon made the decision to go to New Orleans, into the most racist and dangerous state in the union, to fight a white man for the Featherweight Championship of America. But before he undertook this historic fight, Dixon briefly travelled the country with a vaudeville show and took on a title defense against Fred Johnson, who was considered England's best featherweight challenger.

* * *

In the late morning of January 8, 1892, in Shreveport, Louisiana, a plantation lessee named William Driscoll walked toward a shabby, two-room shack located on his property. From inside the shack, a black man named Nathan Andrews watched with growing concern as Driscoll approached.

For reasons not clear, Driscoll had come to order Andrews out.

Andrews refused.

In fear for his life, Andrews pointed a rifle through a crack in the doorjamb and shot Driscoll through the arm. As Driscoll lay bleeding, a frantic Andrews left the house through a back door.

But he did not run far.

Within an hour, a small posse found Andrews in a nearby field and returned him, bound, to the plantation. Not long afterward, Andrews was placed in a wagon and taken on the road to the jail in Shreveport. Along the way, an angry mob of fifty men, shouting and jeering, stopped the wagon. One produced a rope. A passerby, a black man whose name was not recorded, was forced to stop and bear witness.

Andrews was placed astride a white horse and brought beneath the bough of a cottonwood tree. A noose was pulled about Andrews' neck and tied to the bough. The shouting and jeering increased until a signal was given, and one of the men slapped the horse on the rump. The horse bolted and the rope pulled taut, leaving Andrews hanging in the air.

After Andrews died, the forced witness was allowed to leave to spread the word to other blacks.

No one was charged with the killing.

* * *

On March 8, 1892, *The Logansport Daily Pharos* reported that George Dixon and Tom O'Rourke, then travelling with a vaudeville show in Indiana, had checked into the Hotel Genesee for the evening. The next morning, when the two arrived at the hotel restaurant for breakfast, a guest complained to the management about a black man being allowed in their company. Later, at lunch, the manager informed Dixon that he would not be allowed to enter the room. O'Rourke was enraged. He engaged in a heated argument with the manager until the manager relented. The experience was just another humiliation among many that George Dixon stoically faced as he travelled the country. In fact, his wife Kitty would often have to stay in a whites only hotel, while Dixon slept in a blacks only hotel or in the home of a local.

* * *

Some months later, on June 27, 1892, *The Boston Globe* reported that a black man named Thomas Bates was taken forcibly from his jail cell in Shelbyville, Tennessee, by two hundred irate men. Bates was in jail for the confessed killing of his wife, whose throat he had cut "from ear to ear." The mob dragged Bates, kicking and crying, through the dirt street to the base of a gnarled oak tree not thirty yards away. There, with a noose tied around his neck, Bates was hanged.

He died listening to the jeers of the angry crowd.

No one was charged with his killing.

* * *

On the same day Thomas Bates was hanged, George Dixon and Fred Johnson, the English boxing champion, stood opposite each other for their weigh-in before their fight on Coney Island in New York. An inch taller and five years older than Dixon, Fred Johnson had been fighting in England for six years. He was known to be a hard puncher and had risen to the top of the featherweight field with an impressive record of forty-seven wins and three losses.

After the weigh-in, Dixon and O'Rourke made their way to Widow O'Brien's Road House and "ate a hearty dinner." Johnson returned to his training camp and made a meal of a plowman's dinner – muttonchops, toast, and porterhouse steak washed down with a "bottle of Bass Ale and tea." Johnson told a reporter of the Salt Lake City's *Daily Tribune*, "I have come 3,000 miles to meet Dixon, and I do not propose to allow anything to happen to me while in training that might result in my defeat. When I go into the ring, I will be in better condition than I ever was in my life. If Dixon outfights and outgenerals me, he will win, and I will regard him as the greatest boxer of his weight in the world."

At 7:00 p.m., on the night of the Dixon-Johnson fight, the *Police Gazette* reported, "Every train and boat running to Coney Island carried large delegations of sporting men." At 8:00 p.m., John L. Sullivan entered the club, waving. The crowd rose and cheered as he made his way to box seat 42. Not long afterward, his New Orleans opponent, "Gentleman" Jim Corbett, arrived too. An equally deafening cheer was also offered, as he too waved and made his way to box seat 48. He passed Sullivan "without as much as a nod."

The assembled crowd inside the four-storey, wooden warehouse, known as the Coney Island Athletic Club, swelled to more than six thousand. A large illustration in the *Police Gazette* shows men in full suits and bowler hats, waving their arms and cheering. Some are smoking cigarettes and others cigars. A large group of men stand beneath a sign stating in bold lettering, "No Betting Allowed." No doubt the irony of its inclusion was intended; they are furiously betting on the outcome, three to one for Dixon.

After a preliminary bout between two local bantamweights, George Dixon entered the arena in a long bathrobe. He moved swiftly through the crowd to the ring amid great cheers. Behind him followed his seconds, Tom O'Rourke, Maurice Keely, Ed Daly, and timekeeper Mike Bradley. Fifteen minutes later, Fred Johnson entered the arena with his handlers, Charlie Norton, Ben Rowlands, Billy Pilmmer, timekeeper P.J. Donohue, and bottle-holder Benny Murphy. As Johnson stepped into the ring, the crowd roared with enthusiasm.

Referee Al Smith was introduced, and the two combatants shed their robes. Dixon wore a white breechcloth while Johnson wore pale red. The six thousand fans continued to cheer as the referee called the contestants to the centre of the ring. Both fighters listened with care to the instructions. They nodded and shook hands.

At 9:52 p.m., the bell sounded for round one.

Through rounds one and two, the fighters offered little more than cautious probing. In round three, Johnson took the offensive with quick combinations. But Dixon responded to every punch with devastating counterpunches. "The round ended," noted the *Police Gazette*, "with Dixon going to his corner smiling, while Johnson appeared nervous." Johnson adjusted his attack over the next few rounds and was able to land some well-placed blows.

By round eleven both fighters had slowed, showing signs of serious fatigue. Combinations and counterpunches were followed by long clinches in rounds twelve through thirteen.

Finally, in the fourteenth, Dixon saw his opportunity. He struck Johnson with an overhand right on the jaw. Johnson's legs buckled. He fell forward, hitting the "hard boards with terrible force." He tried to rise once but fell back to the canvas at the count of ten. The referee, Al Smith, announced that Dixon was the winner.

The appreciative crowd shouted its approval.

"Good for Boston," John L. Sullivan was heard to yell, "and good for the United States."

* * *

Though Dixon's victory was a great achievement, the fight was not without its portents. *The Boston Globe* described an incident following the fight that revealed a rare example of George Dixon losing his temper in public.

"While fighters have always been found sadly lacking in the art of speechmaking," *The Boston Globe* reported, "some of the more famous sluggers had a knack of expressing themselves forcibly in a very few words. Little George Dixon has always been as mum as the proverbial clam. He was as bashful as a schoolgirl when it came to talking about his deeds in the ring. Dixon made only one speech during his long career, and that one might perhaps be called involuntary at that. Despite his color, 'Little Chocolate' was second only to John L. in popularity. Even his bitterest enemies never referred to his race or color. But last night, after he had whipped Fred Johnson of England at Coney Island, an angry Briton, who had lost heavily in Johnson's defeat, went to the featherweight champion and chastised him." The "angry Briton" had pushed his way through the crowd to Dixon and he accosted him. "You're a bloody nigger!" the Briton shouted, "and I think you deliberately back-heeled Freddie."

Normally agreeable in the most difficult circumstances, Dixon was visibly enraged. He "turned to his detractor, and, with a look of scorn, disgust and rage combined, said in a whisper that could be heard halfway through the box seats, 'I am surprised that they don't teach folks manners in England. I'm sorry Johnson lost, but I had to beat him if I could, because I was defending my title. I'm no 'nigger' and never will be. A 'nigger' is what people call a no-account member of my race. You can go to hell!" The Englishman reportedly slipped quickly and quietly out of the building.

What role the incident played in Dixon's mindset as he made plans for his travel to the Deep South is not known. But he certainly must have internalized each of these experiences and tasted a sour centre in the sweetness of his victories in the ring.

* * *

From New York, George Dixon and Tom O'Rourke travelled back to Boston and then began the long trip to New Orleans for the Carnival of Champions. This event would be a turning point in the history of modern boxing. In his biography of the first black heavyweight champion, Jack Johnson, author Geoffrey C. Ward wrote that the fight between "Gentleman" Jim Corbett and John L. Sullivan "marked the real beginning of the modern boxing era." Ward added, "Instead of meeting in secret in a farmer's field or aboard an anchored offshore barge, they would fight beneath the electrically illuminated roof of an enclosed stadium as the climax of a three-night 'Triple Event' of boxing covered by sportswriters from all over the country."

The fights for the Carnival of Champions were chosen for their premier drawing power. Not only were the bouts meant to showcase boxing, but they were also meant to provide a prime opportunity for unprecedented gambling. So the organizers looked to the greatest fighters of the day in three major weight classes for their event – heavyweight John L. Sullivan, lightweight Jack McAuliffe, and featherweight George Dixon.

Worthy fights were arranged between lightweights Jack McAuliffe and challenger Billy Myer, and between challenger "Gentleman" Jim Corbett and the American heavyweight champion John L. Sullivan. But the organizers were uncertain as to who would be a strong enough opponent for Dixon. As the *Police Gazette* later noted, "Who to get for Dixon … was a puzzle for the club officials. He was the only recognized winner of a world's championship title that America could boast of, and to have a champions' carnival without the colored wonder would have been like the tragedy of Hamlet minus the personage about whom the story revolved."

Conscious of creating advantageous betting odds, the organizers looked for a featherweight challenger Dixon had not already beaten. They accepted an offer from a "zealous and too confident backer" to have a fighter named Jack Skelly take on Dixon. Skelly "had been earning laurels as an amateur" and had won numerous amateur titles. To make the fight more attractive to Dixon, a side wager of $5,000 was offered above the purse of $7,500.

Dixon was drawn to the sizable purse, but he would only agree to the fight if the organizers accepted an additional demand – the setting aside of a thousand seats for local blacks to watch the fight. Certainly, the Carnival of Champions organizers would have been conscious of the empowering message they would send to the black community if they agreed to the condition, and they would have been equally conscious of the ire they would raise among racist whites if they did.

Yet, in the end, they gave Dixon what he wanted.

That the organizers did this says much about the drawing power of George Dixon the boxer and the man at the height of his talent and fame. And in this context, with Dixon's condition being seen as an open, even defiant, call for dignity and solidarity among the black community, the Dixon-Skelly fight in New Orleans represented a significant moment in the long march toward civil rights.

* * *

On the first night of the Carnival of Champions, September 5, 1892, Jack McAuliffe easily knocked out Billy Myer in an uneventful fifteen rounds. Despite the lacklustre fight the fans' enthusiasm was palpable. A *Spokane Review* reporter wrote, "The excitement which has prevailed in this city has had no parallel. There has been no subject of conversation discussed in any quarter save the event of the evening in which every portion of the civilized world is more or less deeply interested."

* * *

Jack Skelly, Dixon's opponent on the evening of September 6, 1892, was born in Brooklyn, New York. He was five feet five inches tall and began fighting in 1888, winning a series of solid but hardly spectacular bouts. In spite of this mediocre record, in the hype-filled preamble to the fight, Skelly was presented to the boxing world as a worthy opponent to Dixon in New Orleans. And in the charged, racist context of New Orleans, many were willing to believe it.

When the Dixon-Skelly match was set some months earlier in the Saint James Hotel in New York, Tom O'Rourke and Billy Reynolds argued for four hours over one pound in the weight limit. It was assumed by both that Skelly would be the heavier man, so they settled on 118 pounds. Yet when the two were finally weighed in New Orleans, it was Dixon who came in at 118 pounds, while Skelly weighed 116½ pounds. All present noted that Skelly was physically fit and presented a fine-looking boxer. But despite the efforts to play up Skelly's strength and skill, it was George Dixon who remained the prohibitive favourite by five to one among the "sports" as fight day approached.

And the betting was heavy.

On the night of the Dixon-Skelly bout, the local newspapers recorded that the evening was comfortably cool. As well, they noted the sky was clear and "the streets [around the Olympic Club] were free from mud and water, and everybody appeared to be in a humor to enjoy the sport." Policemen were stationed throughout the area to keep "a sharp watch for the light-fingered gentry who have come here in considerable numbers from Boston, New York, and Chicago." As the enormous crowd waited to enter, they talked loudly and passionately about the McAuliffe-Myer fight from the night before, and they argued about the relative fighting merits of Skelly and Dixon.

At 7:00 p.m. on September 6, the thousands of fans entered the Olympic Club in New Orleans. The venue was well designed for the affair, and people found their seats with ease. High in the gallery, behind Dixon's corner, noted *The Boston Globe*, were the seats that had been "set apart for the colored men."

"In one way this was the most interesting contest of the two," said *The Boston Globe*, comparing this fight to the Sullivan and Corbett match scheduled for the next evening. "The color line is just as closely drawn in the ring as it is socially here. Many of the Orleanians have sought to criticize the club officials for making a match between a colored man and the white fighter who was deemed his inferior. The matter caused fully as much talk as the [heavyweight] match between Sullivan and Corbett."

At 8:00 p.m., the modern electric lights, installed just for the event, malfunctioned and oil lamps were lit in their place. The representatives of both fighters expressed their concerns about the dimness of the venue. However, the electric lights were finally restored, and all was in good working order.

The reporter for *The Boston Globe* noted the crowd was not as large as it had been the night before. "All the visiting patrons were on hand," he speculated, "but the local patrons who, it was apparent, did not care to see the white man knocked out by a negro, a thing they firmly expected. The effect of such a result, they believed, would make the negro simply unbearable." Then the reporter added, "It would be a local calamity."

At 8:15 p.m., both George Dixon and Jack Skelly arrived, and each was shown to his dressing room. *The Boston Globe* reporter was granted entry to Skelly's room, where he found the fighter being prepared by his seconds. On the wall, the reporter noted a "beautiful embroidered set of colors" which had been given to Skelly by his backer. In one corner of the "colors" was the American flag, and below that, the "harp of Ireland." The initials O.C. were embroidered on the flag for the New York Olympic Club, and a "dart piercing Cupid's heart" had been added as well.

Skelly noticed the reporter looking at the banner. He walked over from his cot and pointed at the heart. "That's the thing I care for more than the others," he said. "Flags don't cut any figure when a case of love is involved." He explained to the reporter that he was fighting to make money for his impending marriage.

In the hall, Captain Barrett of the police entered the ring at 8:30 p.m. He first inspected the ropes and then looked over the crowd. Satisfied that all was as it should be, he left. Soon afterward, local dignitaries arrived and found their seats, while "colored waiters" walked among the patrons nearest to the ring, serving ice water. Spectators looking for beer made their way to the clubhouse. High above, in the galleries, more fans milled about and found their seats. The rumble of conversation grew as the minutes passed.

Upstairs in his dressing room, George Dixon was being rubbed down for the fight. Tom O'Rourke "was as attentive to Dixon as though he had been his own son." When the rubdown was finished, Dixon stood. O'Rourke adjusted Dixon's light-coloured trunks. Then he "folded up the colors which Dixon wore in England in his fight with Nunc Wallace and tied them around his waist." Dixon looked relaxed and ready. He smiled at O'Rourke.

"Do you expect that this will be a long fight?" a reporter in the room asked Dixon.

Dixon's smile grew wider and he winked. "I hardly think that's a fair question," he said. "I'm going into the ring to do the best I can. But I can assure you that the fight won't last very long, if I get this fellow where I want him."

In Skelly's dressing room, one of the attendants discovered that Skelly's trunks had been forgotten. After some minor confusion, Jack McAuliffe, the lightweight who had won the fight the night before, quickly found a replacement pair. "I'm mighty glad to get these, Jack," said an appreciative Skelly, "and if I do as well with them as you did, I'll be the happiest man on earth."

"Why, you will simply punch holes in this fellow," a smiling McAuliffe said. "He's never been punched, and you'll make him feel the gaff."

* * *

At 9:01 p.m., George Dixon entered the ring before nearly ten thousand people and took the same seat that McAuliffe had taken the night before. The "colored spectators" registered their approval with deafening applause. A moment later, Skelly entered the ring also to the vocal approval of the crowd. He smiled and waved as he took his stool in the ring.

At 9:07 p.m., Dixon and Skelly were called to the centre of the ring to hear instructions and to shake hands.

Less than a minute later, the bell sounded and the first round was underway.

Each fighter moved about the ring with caution, until the nervous Skelly made his move. He threw a roundhouse right swing at Dixon's jaw. At that same moment, Dixon let loose a sharp left to Skelly's mouth. Both punches landed, and the fighters clinched.

Referee Duffy separated them.

Again, Skelly took the charge, with a right at Dixon's head. But Dixon deftly sidestepped, and the swing went wide. Skelly followed with another punch, only to be met with a quicker right counterpunch to the mouth. Skelly leaned in and clinched again. Using a free hand, Dixon pounded at Skelly's ribs. When they pulled away, Skelly caught Dixon weakly in the jaw. The two danced around each other, sparring lightly for the remainder of the round, though the strength of Dixon's talent and tactics was clear.

In round two, Skelly, wary of Dixon's counterpunches, danced away as Dixon tried to get in. But Dixon was quick, stepping forward and throwing a straight right. Skelly ducked under it and leaned into another clinch.

Dixon broke away and attacked, but missed with both punches of a head combination. The two backed away, dancing and sparring. Dixon noted how Skelly guarded his head, so he changed tactics. He moved in but directed his attack at Skelly's stomach and ribs. Then he stepped to the right and swung a hard left that connected with Skelly's gut. Skelly slumped, and the crowd groaned. And before Skelly could correct his defenses, Dixon returned with another right to the ribs.

Skelly was stunned.

Before Skelly could move Dixon delivered yet another left to the stomach. Skelly moved to counter, offering a feeble jab to Dixon's face. Then the two fell into another clinch. When they broke, Skelly regrouped and offered more disciplined, effective punches, ending with a quick combination to Dixon's face.

Dixon countered with a left to Skelly's face, but Skelly ducked under the punch and turned his right shoulder forward, catching Dixon on the ear. Dixon countered with a left to the stomach and a right to the neck, to which many in the dismayed crowed yelled, "Foul!" Dixon stepped back and motioned an apology. Skelly curtly nodded. Dixon returned to the attack, throwing a left to Skelly's chest, which grew "rapidly rosy and puffed" from Dixon's repeated punches. Skelly retreated. Dixon pressed. At the bell, Skelly's nose began to swell.

Skelly came out sharply at the round three bell, pushing Dixon back to the ropes. But Dixon would not be caught in the corner and he danced away, throwing a left hand to Skelly's ribs and a right to his jaw, which soundly rattled him.

Skelly dropped to a knee but rose quickly.

Dixon pounced and delivered two more punches before the overwhelmed Skelly leaned forward and clinched. When the two broke apart, Dixon shot two rights to the ribs, forcing Skelly back. Dixon, in pursuit, levelled a left at Skelly's jaw and a right to his ribs. Skelly countered with two good strikes to Dixon's head, but Dixon shrugged the blows off, delivering yet another shot to Skelly's ribs.

Despite Skelly's efforts to slow the pace, Dixon relentlessly attacked Skelly's ribs, heart, and jaw. And each time Skelly clinched to avoid more blows, Dixon offered more punishment to his ribs.

Only the bell ending round three saved Skelly.

In round four, Skelly repeated his tactic of round three, charging at Dixon. But Dixon kept his distance, waiting for chances. When he saw an opening, he stepped in and struck a left-hand blow to Skelly's stomach. Skelly countered with a weak jab that missed. He tried to corner Dixon, but Dixon would have none of it, dancing away at the last moment, delivering yet another blow to Skelly's chest.

Skelly and Dixon clinched. They broke. Dixon struck Skelly on the nose, and Skelly responded with a left to Dixon's temple, only to have Dixon throw a punch to his stomach and two quick strikes to the now visibly bruised ribs. Skelly tried a swing at Dixon's ear. He connected, but weakly, and was then stunned by a Dixon left to his mouth. Skelly staggered, his hands held high to protect his face. Dixon took the opening and punished Skelly in the stomach and ribs.

So it continued until the bell.

Finding a second wind, Skelly bounded from his corner to start round five. The two fighters jabbed and probed until Dixon found his target with a hard right on Skelly's ribs. They fell into a clinch. As they broke, Dixon offered a weak shot to Skelly's jaw, to which Skelly, perhaps confused, pulled into another clinch. When again they broke, Dixon was sharper with his delivery and landed a straight right hand on Skelly's nose and mouth. Skelly began to bleed, and staggered into a clinch for a moment. But Dixon was quick to break and throw a terrific left to Skelly's jaw. Skelly turned away from the punch only to catch Dixon's right above the left eye. A gash immediately opened and blood "flowed freely."

Skelly was now desperate and threw his arms around Dixon's neck. But Dixon danced back and offered another shot to Skelly's eye, widening the cut and increasing the blood flow, which now ran down Skelly's face, neck, and chest. Dixon would not let up and delivered another right to the jaw and left to the neck. Skelly fell back against the ropes, holding his hands near his face, making feeble efforts to counter, until finally the bell rang.

* * *

While the fight progressed in New Orleans, police in Atlanta, Georgia, were busy cutting down the bodies of three black men – John Ransom, Jack Walker, and Bill Armer – who had been lynched on a tree limb that reached out over a road. The locals would later say the killings were the result of a "race war." Though the story was never clear, a party of twenty or thirty armed and masked men had entered the home of Jack Walker and dragged the three into the street, where they were beaten, tortured, and hanged.

No one was charged with the killings.

* * *

At the start of round six, Dixon charged the bloodied and bruised Skelly, throwing quick combinations. Skelly made a good series of parries and counterpunches. Then, to the cheers of the crowd, he took charge and forced Dixon back into a corner. Dixon slipped to the side, offering a shot to Skelly's stomach for his troubles. Skelly threw a punch at Dixon's eye. Dixon responded with a hard right. Skelly ducked, only to catch a Dixon left uppercut full on the mouth.

Skelly backed up with Dixon in pursuit. He hit Skelly in the neck with a right as Skelly countered with a left to the jaw. Dixon was unfazed. He shot back with a left over Skelly's guard, causing a new gash to open below the eye. Skelly tried a left to Dixon's nose, but Dixon countered with a thunderous left uppercut to Skelly's heart. Skelly fell back only to have Dixon press on, landing an overhand right that snapped Skelly's head back. The two then clinched in a "bear hug."

When they parted, Dixon stepped forward with a left to Skelly's neck. Skelly struck Dixon with a left to the ear. Dixon reeled.

The crowd roared.

Dixon recovered and landed two hard lefts to Skelly's nose. Skelly stepped closer and delivered a left and right combination to Dixon's head, while Dixon managed a close-in jab at Skelly's nose. The two fell once more into a clinch until the bell rang. Though Skelly had shown more life in the round, he bled profusely. Dixon, observed many, still looked no worse for wear.

Skelly was unsteady as he came up for round seven and clinched at the first opportunity. When they parted, Dixon landed a left-hand jab to Skelly's jaw, then struck at his ribs and jaw. Skelly defended well until Dixon landed a stinging right hand to his eye. Skelly reeled and nearly went down. Dixon followed with a right to the jaw and a left uppercut to the chest. Skelly wobbled then dropped to his knees. He rose unsteadily only to have Dixon knock him down again with a right to the jaw. Once more Skelly rose and clinched. When they parted, Dixon caught Skelly on the right ear. Skelly was so groggy and disoriented by the bell that Captain Barrett of the New Orleans Police stepped to the ringside prepared to stop the fight.

Skelly refused, and the fight continued.

The police captain looked uncertain as Skelly left his corner for round eight. Dixon smiled at Skelly, who lunged and missed with an awkward swing. Dixon stepped aside and managed a quick left to Skelly's head before the two clinched. When Skelly broke, he rushed at Dixon, but Dixon sidestepped and countered with a sharp uppercut. Dixon pushed Skelly back and delivered a right to the neck and left uppercut to the ribs. Skelly sank into the ropes, helpless. Dixon pressed on, delivering one combination after another. Somehow, Skelly found the strength to slip away. Dixon followed, forcing him again into the ropes. Skelly managed to defend against the blows, but his arms grew heavy. Dixon caught Skelly with a left to the jaw, and Skelly dropped to the canvas. Again, he rose. Dixon feigned with a left and then shot a right blow to the jaw. Skelly fell again to his knees, then he rolled heavily away to his back.

His head hit the canvas hard.

He was out.

Some in the crowd cheered, while most offered their vocal disgust. Afraid of reprisals, Dixon quickly made his way to his dressing room.

* * *

Two burly policemen stood outside Skelly's dressing room where, inside, two physicians attended to him. He was covered in red marks on his body, and his nose was "swollen to almost twice its natural size, and the bridge was fractured and bleeding." When Skelly found the strength, he spoke with the reporter from *The Boston Globe*. "I want you to send something to New York for me. I am very sorry for my friends who bet on me, and I will do anything in my power to square up with them. I fought as well as I could, but it did not take me long to find out that I had underestimated Dixon's pugilistic ability. I do not believe that I ever hit Dixon, now that I come to think of it. He was entirely too fast for me."

With tears in his eyes, Skelly shook his head.

"I would never have entered this fight," he continued, "if it had not been that I wanted to get enough money to start in shape, as I am to marry, but now

I don't know what I will do. I shall never forgive myself for making this match, not because I was whipped, as that does not bother me a bit. As far as the pain and that sort of thing goes, I can stand that very well, but I know a great many of my friends in Brooklyn, who could not well afford to risk their dollars, backed me for friendship's sake. That is the bitter pill for me." His seconds helped dress him, then Skelly had a bottle of ale, which helped him "regain his spirits."

* * *

The papers that covered the fight noted the angry racism. "White fans winced," wrote the reporter for the *Chicago Tribune*, "every time Dixon landed on Skelly. The sight was repugnant to some of the men from the South. A darky is alright in his place here, but the idea of sitting quietly by and seeing a colored boy pommel a white lad grates on Southerners."

The comments in other papers were subtler. "What with bruises, lacerations, and coagulated blood," wrote the reporter for the New Orleans *Times-Democrat*, "Skelly's nose, mouth, and eye presented a horrible spectacle. Some even turned away their heads in disgust, at that face already disfigured past recognition."

And the New Orleans *Daily Picayune* did not miss the larger significance of what Dixon had done that evening. "It was a mistake to match a negro and a white man," read the paper, "a mistake to bring the races together on any terms of equality, even in the prize ring. It was not pleasant to see a white man applaud a negro for knocking another white man out."

The *Times-Democrat* agreed. "We sincerely trust that this mistake – for it was a mistake and a serious one to match a negro with a white man – will not be repeated," ran the editorial on September 8, 1892. "For among the ignorant negroes the idea has naturally been created that it was a test of strength and fighting power of Caucasian and African ... which give negroes false ideas and dangerous beliefs ... And the white race of the south will destroy itself if it tolerates equality of any kind."

Four days later, the same group that had organized the boxing festival, the Olympic Athletic Club, decided to suspend bouts between black and white boxers – a ban that would last a generation.

A year after the fight, the *Police Gazette* noted on September 30, 1893, "Nearly every time Dixon has been pitted against a champion, no matter whether foreign or native, the majority has named Dixon the loser, probably through prejudice, owing to his color, yet he has won."

The northern black press was also well aware of the fight's significance. "Dixon has given a favorite Dixie prejudice a black eye," reported the *Cleveland Gazette*. "It is all right to see a white man whip another in the south, but to pay one's dollars and a number of them, too, to see a Hamite 'whip the stuffing out of' a white man, even if he is a northerner, and then give the former an ovation, is something more than the average southerner can or will stand." With pride the paper added, "My! But how heavy Dixon's victory must have sat on their delicate stomachs!"

Years later Dixon's defeat of Skelly in the Deep South was still remembered as a racial upset. "Some of the old-timers tell about the time George Dixon, described as the whitest black man who ever stepped inside the ropes, knocked out Jack Skelly in New Orleans," began a short article in the January 24, 1916, edition of *The Day*, published in New London, Connectcut. "It was along about the seventh round that Dixon, after he teased Jack from the start, slipped over the sleep punch. Tom O'Rourke saw it coming and was ready for it, for almost before the referee had finished the count over Skelly's prostrate form, O'Rourke pulled the smoke through the ropes, rushed him away from the crowd and wasn't seen in New Orleans again for several moons. It is likely the mob of southerners would have given Dixon some rough treatment if they had located him that night."

* * *

On the third night of the Carnival of Champions, September 7, 1892, John L. Sullivan fought Jim Corbett in a match that, for all its hype, was decidedly one-sided. Sullivan at thirty-three was slow and overweight after months of overeating and excessive drinking. From the eighth round on, he wheezed audibly and struggled desperately to keep up with the defensive-minded Corbett. Corbett easily countered all of Sullivan's clumsy lunges with sharp, well-placed punches, until finally John L. Sullivan, the first heavyweight champion of the gloved era, simply collapsed in the twenty-first round.

He had lost the fight.

It was a painful end for the first giant of modern boxing. After the knockout count, Sullivan struggled to the ropes, and then to his feet. He looked to the crowd and delivered a heartfelt, impromptu farewell. No doubt, Dixon, who had fought the night before, witnessed the fight and listened to Sullivan's speech. "Gentlemen," said the exhausted John L. to the crowd, "all I have to say is that I came into the ring once too often. And if I had to get licked, I'm glad to say, I was licked by an American. I remain your warm personal friend, John L. Sullivan."

The crowd cheered the champion's farewell.

"Sullivan was morose," reported *The New York Times* the next day, "and had been imbibing enough to make him sleep till noon and render him stupid all the afternoon." The result of the match was tinged with irony. The Carnival of Champions had inaugurated a new era for boxing by legitimizing the sport, while at the same time it finished the career of its first great practitioner.

While fans busily lauded the new champion, "Gentleman" Jim Corbett, John L. Sullivan was left nearly alone. After the fight, he returned to his dressing room where he "threw himself on a lounge and broke down entirely. His self-control was gone, and in a moment he was blubbering like a child." His seconds and attendants did their best to cheer him. But Sullivan was inconsolable, beaten emotionally as well as physically. "His upper lip was bruised and swollen to twice its natural size," noted *The New York Times*. "There were splotches of red where Corbett had sent home that clever, vicious left, and the nose was cut and bleeding. It was a repulsive face. The sneer around the corner of the mouth was gone, and the countenance had lost its ferocity."

Sullivan wept openly as he spoke to the reporter. "I did not feel him but once," John L. said. "The punishment did not hurt me early in the night. It was only in the last round that he troubled me. When he smashed me in the face, then I felt as though I was falling backward off a bridge into water, and after that I don't remember anything."

Sullivan could say no more and again began weeping. When he pulled himself together, he turned to one of his backers in the room. "Charley," he said, "I'm sorry you backed me and lost your money.

"Never mind, John," answered Charley. "I don't mind the money. It's gone, and what's gone is lost. Nobody can lick you but Corbett, and you are better than

[Charlie] Mitchell. When the Englishman wants to fight you, my money is at hand." A waiter then entered the room and handed Sullivan a brandy.

"It only loosened his tongue," said the embarrassed *New York Times* reporter, "and made him sob more."

Whether George Dixon visited John L. Sullivan that night is unrecorded. But he must have been aware, as few others possibly could have been aware, of the crushing weight of disappointment and loss that Sullivan felt. And perhaps, standing as he did at the pinnacle of his boxing career, Dixon made the briefest note of how quickly the fall can come.

*

In late October 1892, a young black man named Allen Parker was arrested and charged in Monroe County, Alabama, with "burning a gin house and fifteen bales of cotton." When Parker asked what evidence there was of his guilt, the deputy sheriff said he had a "witness." So the sheriff bound Parker and carried him in a wagon to the Monroeville jail. Two miles from the town, twenty men took the sheriff by surprise and held him down while others elicited a confession from Parker. The terrified Parker was then tied to a tree and hanged, not far from where, two weeks earlier, four other black men were hanged for an alleged murder.

No one was charged with any of the killings.

PART II
THE FALL

Round Seven

Guard For Cross Counter Blow: *There are three different ways known to science of the present day to avoid a cross counter blow. The first and most common being to duck the head. The second by placing the right hand on the left side of the face. The third by shifting the left arm, immediately after striking the blow, directly opposite the position in which it lands. Cut No. 6 shows a guard for cross counter by shifting the left arm into the shape of the letter V turned upside down. This last guard is decidedly the safest way to avoid a cross counter blow, for while ducking the head you are liable to be hit with a left hand uppercut, and if you place the right hand on the left side of your face, you are compelled to leave your body entirely unguarded. I usually obtain better results by shifting the arm and accordingly prefer to use and recommend it.*

— George Dixon, "A Lesson in Boxing" (1893)

In early 1893, railroad speculation triggered the worst economic depression in the United States prior to 1929. Within a year of the railroad stock collapse, estimates of unemployment in the United States ran as high as eighteen percent and would remain over ten percent for nearly three years. During the winter of that first year, thousands starved and thousands more wandered the country looking for work. Violent labour conflicts ensued – the Carnegie Steel Works Strike and the Chicago Pullman Strike among the most infamous. Such economic strife made the already contentious divisions between class and race in America even worse.

And this was reflected in the boxing ring.

* * *

In July of 1893, nearly a year after the Carnival of Champions, George Dixon, Tom O'Rourke, and likely Kitty Dixon travelled together to Chicago to see the World's Fair – the Columbian Exhibition. How they spent their time and what they saw is uncertain, but they must have enjoyed themselves. George Dixon had achieved a level of success unmatched in boxing.

After his fight with Jack Skelly, Dixon defended his title nearly twenty times without a single loss against the best fighters in New York, Philadelphia, and Washington. He fought the formidable Walter "Kentucky Rosebud" Edgerton four times, drawing the first two and winning the next two. He also fought in numerous exhibition fights. He was flush with money and filled with the confidence of long success, with steady offers for more lucrative fights still to come.

The future seemed full with promise.

The clear title of champion had been bestowed on Dixon by no less than the editor of the *Police Gazette*, the unofficial arbiter of such matters in boxing. Against continued claims that Dixon was not the featherweight and bantamweight champion, editor Richard K. Fox wrote, "Dixon is entitled to the high honors [featherweight and bantamweight champion] that O'Rourke claims for him and the *Police Gazette* will back that claim to the limit."

Dixon was now entering a new phase of his boxing career, no longer chasing the respect due to an up-and-comer, and no longer pursuing the acclaim due to a champion. He was cashing in. Since professional athletes of that time did not have endorsements to augment their winnings (though they could bet on their own fights as an alternate means of income), it was common for boxing champions to tour in the vaudeville circuit for a healthy addition to their income. John L. Sullivan had established the model. The champion would gather together performers of all kinds for a travelling roadshow – dancers, singers, jugglers, and comics. Central to the entire performance, of course, was an exhibition bout by the champion against all comers.

Dixon, never one to miss such a lucrative financial opportunity, was quick to follow in Sullivan's footsteps.

An advertisement for Dixon's vaudeville troupe ran in the *Lowell Daily Sun* on Wednesday, November 22, 1893. "Lowell Opera House, One Night, Wednesday, November 22. George Dixon's Vaudeville and Specialty Company. Our lists of Artists – Binns and Burns, Musical Artists. Byron and Evens, two Comedians. Kitty Nelson, Song and Dance Artist, and Champion Lady Swing and Buck Dancer of America. Wills & Barton, Comedy Duo. Van and Lesley, Refined Sketch Artists. Maliel Guver, the Vital Spark. Patterson Bros., Kings of the Horizontal Bars. Murphy and McCoy, Irish Comedians. Sisters Aleene, introducing the Gauze Dance. Prof. Jack Lynch of Philadelphia, Sparring Partner of George Dixon. George Dixon, Champion Featherweight of the World, will meet all comers in his class and forfeit $50 to any man he does not outpoint in 4 rounds. 75, 50, 35, 25, 10 cents."

That night, "a fair sized audience ... comprised principally of men gathered at the Opera house to see George Dixon, the champion featherweight pugilist, and a clever variety show." The variety show was well reviewed, but the main event of the evening was the four-round demonstration with Tom Moriarty of Lowell. It was to be a "scientific contest for points ... and should a knock-out blow be delivered, it will be by accident." The four rounds were a clever exercise in dodging. The crowed cheered enthusiastically with each blow.

These vaudevillian shows were wildly popular among boxing fans, but they could also invite trouble. Just a day after the performance in Lowell, Massachusetts, for instance, Dixon found himself in the Lawrence Police Court being fined $100 by Judge Stone for "assault on a 'soft shelled slugger' of that town who wanted to stand up before Dixon." Noted the newspaper, "The defendant appealed."

* * *

Not long after Dixon earned his title, and perhaps, in part, because he had achieved his great goals, Dixon fell into a period of drift. His disciplined attention to the boxing craft wavered as he looked to increase his income in the vaudeville circuit. And with that life came greater engagement in the sporting life. "After winning the featherweight title," wrote Nat Fleischer of Dixon, "wine, women and song were sweet music to his ears." In Boston, Dixon frequented the local saloons. So, too, in the San Juan Hill section of Manhattan, between 59th and 65th Streets, Dixon revelled in the nightlife of the sports community.

Although always free with his money, Dixon increasingly became a notable spendthrift. At the start of a given week, after a major fight, he would have earned thousands of dollars, "only to find it necessary before the week was over to borrow enough money to get him through." He became an "inveterate player of the ponies," though "he lost more than he won." He also "purchased horseflesh," and was said to have owned "a number of good trotters and wasted considerable money on them."

Dixon was also uncommonly generous. "Many an orphan and widow had cause to remember his charity," wrote Nat Fleischer, "for like the immortal John L., he gave freely when requests for charity were made." So, too, Dixon was conscious of being a prominent black man in late-nineteenth century America. "He was a bona-fide good Samaritan to impecunious fellows of his own race," added Fleischer, "his hand always being in his pocket when appeals were made from colored folk with hard luck stories. He also contributed large sums to Negro missions and to schemes for improving conditions of colored people both at home and abroad."

* * *

Dixon's second professional loss came as a surprise. "The other bout [after George Wright in 1889] which was decided against me," recalled Dixon in late 1893, "was with Billy Plimmer of England who was given a decision on points in a four round glove contest which took place at Madison Square Garden, New York City, a few nights after I defeated Eddie Pierce. I will refrain from saying anything further about this contest for reasons which I cannot publicly state."

The fight with Plimmer occurred on August 22, 1893. Billy Plimmer claimed the English bantamweight 110-pound championship. It was said before the fight that Dixon did not train as hard as he might, because he felt Plimmer would not put up much resistance. Besides, thought Dixon, he had won a decisive fight two weeks earlier, on August 7, against Eddie Pierce in three rounds. In his mind, his fitness could not have been too diminished.

After three preliminary, four-round bouts between other fighters, Dixon and Plimmer entered the arena. Dixon slipped through the ropes and into the ring first, receiving a hearty roar of approval from the crowd. He waved and made his way to his corner. Plimmer then arrived, and he too received a "big reception" as he entered through the ropes and into the ring. Dixon smiled as the referee discussed the rules, while Plimmer maintained a "determined look upon his countenance."

When the bell rang, Dixon attacked, "eager to knock out Plimmer." He threw a series of well-executed combinations, but Plimmer proved quicker, sidestepping the assault. The two mixed and clinched then broke. Plimmer landed a left on Dixon's chest. Dixon responded, only to have Plimmer dodge. Plimmer then delivered a combination left to Dixon's chest and right to his neck. When the first round bell rang, it was clear that Dixon was surprised by Plimmer.

Round two saw Dixon move to the centre. He was still smiling, but offered a more determined attack. Yet it was Plimmer who took the charge. Dixon swung for Plimmer's neck, but Plimmer got well inside the punch. When Dixon pulled back, Plimmer delivered a straight left to Dixon's neck. "This rattled Dixon," noted *The Boston Globe* reporter. In response, Dixon swung at

Plimmer's jaw and missed. He then rushed forward and caught Plimmer on the jaw with his right. The audience, expecting Dixon to overwhelm Plimmer, became fully engaged now and excited by the uncertainty. "Bedlam," said the reporter, "was let loose in the building." The cheers and jeers became louder as Plimmer jabbed his left into Dixon's stomach, then slipped away before Dixon could respond.

Plimmer now smiled.

"His grin was wicked," noted the reporter.

Sensing an opportunity, Plimmer pressed the attack, striking Dixon's ribs with a right and his cheek with a left. The sound of the crowd grew even louder. Dixon tried to respond, but he missed with wild swings. "He was very badly mixed up," noted the reporter.

Then for a brief stretch, Dixon rallied. He landed a straight left on Plimmer's mouth and sidestepped Plimmer's counter. Plimmer then landed a left to the neck. But when the bell rang, it was still clear to all that Plimmer had the best of it.

Round three saw Dixon trying to make up for two lost rounds. He swung hard to Plimmer's jaw only to have Plimmer again slip away. Dixon rushed in and caught Plimmer on the neck with both his right and left. Plimmer countered to the jaw. Dixon worked the ribs in a combination.

Then the two fell into a clinch.

When they broke, they stood toe to toe and exchanged blows. And, again, they clinched. This time when they broke, Plimmer struck Dixon so hard in the face, Dixon's head snapped back.

He was rattled.

He swung wildly but missed Plimmer. "The crowd looked on in wonderment," wrote the reporter. Dixon cornered Plimmer and struck with combinations to the head and chest, only to have Plimmer counterpunch with an equally good combination. Both fighters were soon exhausted and fell into a clinch that the referee had to break.

When the bell rang, Plimmer had again outfought Dixon.

At the start of round four, Dixon approached Plimmer with an expression of dead seriousness. He tried two quick strikes to Plimmer's head but missed both. He swung his left, connecting with Plimmer's cheek. Then the "fists flew as fast as bullets in battle." Plimmer landed a right on Dixon's cheek, Dixon a left on Plimmer's ribs. More punches were thrown. Many were dodged. As the time ticked down, Dixon grew increasingly wild, missing with great swings from the left and right. After one missed blow, Plimmer countered with a right so hard it knocked Dixon back. Dixon leaned against the ropes as Plimmer raced forward to finish the job.

Only the bell stopped the unrelenting assault.

While the fighters walked to their corners, Referee O'Donnell announced that Plimmer was the winner. Plimmer jumped in the air, overjoyed. He ran over to Dixon, shook his hand, and said "something pleasant." Dixon was "well-behaved," wrote the reporter, "as he always is, [and] smiled pleasantly in return." Chaos broke out amid the crowd. Many rushed into the ring. Some congratulated the referee for "the justice of his verdict." Others swarmed Plimmer. Some even "picked him up, threw him from one to the other, patted him, hugged him, kissed him on the forehead and cheeks, pulled his ears and told him he was the greatest little man in the world."

Twenty-five police officers cleared a path, and Plimmer was carried on shoulders into the crowd. More than two hundred people remained in the ring where they "tore down the stout, wooden posts, six inches thick, in the excess of their crazy joy." They "howled and cheered."

Shocked and disappointed, George Dixon moved slowly through the crowd and into his dressing room. Since the fight was not "to the finish," the result did not affect Dixon's featherweight title. "Dixon's defeat," wrote the *Police Gazette*, "in no way detracts from Dixon's reputation as regards the championship of featherweights, for he still retains that title as the battle was not to the finish." In the minds of many, however, the loss suggested that, for the first time, George Dixon, the bantamweight and featherweight champion of the world, was finally vulnerable.

* * *

Two days later, Tom O'Rourke sent a letter to the *Police Gazette*. "Since the 4-round boxing contest between Billy Plimmer and George Dixon," he wrote, "I understand that Plimmer believes he can defeat Dixon, and his admirers are also confident that he can do so. I will match the featherweight champion of the world to fight Plimmer at 114 pounds for $5,000 or $10,000 for the *Police Gazette* featherweight belt and the featherweight championship of the world. To prove I mean business, I have posted $1,000 and will agree that the fight shall take place any time suitable to the club offering the largest purse. I allow the weighting to take place at 1 p.m. because I do not want to overtax Dixon, who is fighting below his weight. If Plimmer's backer covers the $1,000 I have posted and names a day to meet, the match can be arranged without any trouble, as both Dixon and myself mean business, and the $1,000 posted proves it."

Plimmer was no fool. Knowing he had more to gain by not fighting Dixon "to the finish," he declined the offer.

* * *

Just a month later, Dixon took on Solly Smith, a promising up-and-coming featherweight, in a proper title defense. The fight was set for a $9,000 purse, the winner taking home $8,000. The fight went on for seven rounds, with exciting exchanges and even notable threats by the challenger. Yet, in the end, Dixon won the bout by a technical knockout. Dixon was pleased with this victory, but he noted the considerable skill of the young Smith.

He had a sense they would meet again.

* * *

In December 1893, Dixon took on "Torpedo" Billy Murphy in Paterson, New Jersey. The fight was lopsided, with Dixon winning easily. The most entertaining moment of the fight came when referee James Stoddard separated Dixon and Murphy in a third-round clinch. Murphy pulled free, turned, and inadvertently struck Stoddard on the nose. Infuriated, Stoddard responded by delivering two quick blows to Murphy, who then clinched with the referee. Dixon, no doubt amused by the sudden change of events, leaned against the ropes and watched until the local police captain stepped into the ring and, acting as the referee, separated Murphy and Stoddard. Murphy was disqualified.

In mid-February 1894, Dixon found himself in court again, this time charged with assault and battery, a crime he was alleged to have committed in Lawrence, when Dixon's vaudeville troupe came to town. Patrick J.

Hennessy took the stand and explained that during the troupe's tour of Lawrence, Dixon announced he would meet all comers in a four-round bout for points. Hennessy volunteered to engage in the bout. He expected "glory and a little money as a result of his go." But it did not turn out that way.

"He punches hard," said Hennessy and claimed Dixon had injured him. When he argued with Dixon after the show, explained Hennessey, Dixon ignored his concerns. So Hennessey contacted the police. The lower court found against Dixon, so Dixon made an appeal, which he lost.

He paid his $100 fine.

In February, Dixon fought a charity bout in Lowell, Massachusetts, and later sparred for charity at a casino in New York in October.

On one evening around this time, while performing in New York's Bowery, Dixon got into a disagreement with Tom O'Rourke. O'Rourke lost his temper and swung at Dixon, striking him in the face. Rather than strike back, Dixon walked away and considered dropping O'Rourke as his manager. His friends talked Dixon out of it. If O'Rourke would shake hands first, said Dixon, he would forget the incident. O'Rourke did. But Dixon never forgot.

The long-standing relationship was showing outward signs of strain.

* * *

Dixon faced his first knockdown in March of 1894 during an exhibition bout with Walter "Kentucky Rosebud" Edgerton. Edgerton was a promising young black fighter who had arranged an exhibition fight with Dixon as part of a fundraising effort for the poor of Philadelphia.

Dixon had been unwell after his long trip to the city, and the two fighters agreed they would spar gently.

During the second round, seeing an opportunity for easy fame, Edgerton ignored the agreement. When Dixon lowered his hands, Edgerton struck hard at Dixon with a left, which Dixon parried, only to be caught by a subsequent right to the neck. "Dixon," noted the *Middletown Daily Argus*, "went down like a log, his head striking the floor a hard crack, which probably stunned him."

More than twenty thousand dumbfounded spectators at the Philadelphia Industrial Hall watched the referee pick Dixon up and sit him in his corner chair. It took a full minute and a half before Dixon "realized what had happened." Dixon was still able to finish the scheduled three rounds and would deny that Edgerton had fairly knocked him down.

Later in the month, Edgerton issued another challenge to Dixon. "Seeing that George Dixon, the featherweight champion, denies that he was knocked out by me when we boxed in Philadelphia on March 22, I wish to state that he was out, for he was unconscious for nearly five minutes, and 10 minutes elapsed before the third round commenced. I could have knocked him out in the third round, but my backer James McHale would not allow me to do so. Now to settle the question, I will fight George Dixon at 118 pounds for $2,500 to $5,000 a side and the featherweight championship of the world, and I will be ready to meet Dixon and his backer at the *Police Gazette* office on Wednesday, April 4, at 11 a.m., to post deposit and sign articles, if O'Rourke accepts this challenge. Should O'Rourke not accept, I shall claim the featherweight championship, and stand ready to fight any man in the world [for] the title."

Dixon was furious and wanted to settle the matter. So the match was arranged for May 7, 1894. The result was predictably anti-climactic. Dixon won the bout decisively in four rounds.

* * *

By early 1894, Dixon had reached a level of success few in boxing had or ever would find. His life as champion and with Kitty seemed the very definition of success. The two owned a large house in fashionable Malden, just north of Boston, said to be worth more than $10,000, a staggering sum, and Dixon had spent a good deal more on it. *The Boston Globe* reported he would return from his fights and retire with a cigar to his "favorite room" there, where he collected "rare works of art and bric-a-brac, and books of which he is very fond." Dixon was "possessed of a large amount of intelligence and [was] very fond of reading," his favourite author being Charles Dickens.

* * *

In June of 1894, George Dixon took on another Australian – Albert Griffiths, who fought under the name Young Griffo. Griffo was a square-jawed tough from Millers Point in New South Wales. He "was not known as much of a puncher, but his skill was uncanny," noted the *Tacoma Daily News*. "He had wonderful headwork, almost impenetrable defense, dazzling feints, and a rapid two-handed method of attack. The cleverest boxers and hardest punchers were made to look ridiculous when exchanging with him. He had a dislike for training and was deemed lazy. [And] there were times he got drunk before a match."

Dixon would face Young Griffo three times, each proving a pitched battle. Their first fight in Boston ended in a twenty-round draw. They fought again in January 1895, on Coney Island, drawing again after twenty-five rounds. And finally, they drew for a third time, in October of 1895, after ten rounds.

Dixon was finding the up-and-coming challengers more difficult to defeat.

Two contemporary drawings show the Dixon-Griffo fight on Coney Island. In the first, a man with long sideburns and a mustache, dressed in a policeman's uniform, weighs the gloves. Beside him, two other men, no doubt the boxers' representatives, look at the scales intently. In the second drawing, the two fighters are shown engaged in the ring. Dixon throws a straight left at Griffo's chin, while Griffo counters with a weak right to Dixon's jaw. The referee, wearing a tie and coat, darts behind them to avoid their movement. Hundreds of men, most wearing bowler hats and mustaches, watch with various states of enthusiasm. Some are shouting while others appear to be gambling.

Young Griffo was well-known for his drinking and rough behaviour on the town after a fight. Not long after their second bout, Griffo came across Dixon in a New York saloon. Griffo was already drunk and low on money, so he pressed George for a loan. Dixon, never one to refuse such a request from a fellow boxer, offered him $150. Griffo took the money and headed out to continue drinking. Not an hour later he returned, having spent $50. He started complaining in front of Dixon and his friends about "the rotten deals he got in his two ring combats with Dixon." Dixon just laughed. In a fit of rage, Griffo took the remaining $100 from his pocket and laid it on the bar, betting he could defeat Dixon in a fight then and there. Again, Dixon laughed. By this point the bar owner had called in a "burly Irish cop," who sent Griffo into the street.

"What do you think of that," laughed Dixon to his friends. "Only this afternoon I gave up one hundred and fifty bucks to mister Griffo, on a quick touch. And here he comes around wanting to fight me with my own money."

In August of 1894, Dixon and a friend drove along a quiet stretch of road from Boston to his home in Malden. The carriage was stopped by three "highwaymen" who emerged from the bushes. One of the men grabbed hold of Dixon's horse and "began to torment the animal." Dixon, still seated in the carriage, calmly told the men to stop. They laughed and began calling him names. Finally, Dixon lost his temper and stepped down from the carriage. When the first of the men tried to attack him, Dixon dropped him with one punch. A second tried his luck and found himself in the same position. Dixon then chased after the third until all three ran off.

Through the remainder of 1894 and into the first half of 1895, Dixon travelled widely with his vaudeville troupe, fighting in exhibition bouts once or twice each evening. Along the way, he defended his title in Wilmington, Philadelphia, Coney Island, New York City, and Louisville against Joe Flynn, Billy Whistler, Young Griffo, Sam Bolen, and Charles Slusher, drawing in two fights and winning three.

In the evenings, after his fights, Dixon took to spending his time in town, carousing with the local sports, drinking and gambling. It seems unlikely that Kitty was travelling with him through this period, as he now spent increasing amounts of time away from home. His drinking and gambling and carousing must have caused considerable strain on their marriage, though again this is uncertain. What is certain, though, is that Dixon's habits outside the ring were chipping away at his positive public persona.

On May 18, 1895, *The New York Times* reported that Dixon had been arrested in Grand Central Station in New York City for being "drunk and disorderly." He was on his way back to Boston with friends when, under the influence of liquor, he walked into the "parlor car, where the women were." Dixon then "made a beastly exhibition of himself," being "profane and boisterous, and scared the women." It was also said that he annoyed passengers in the cars of the Shore Line express. The train had left at 1:00 p.m. and caused "considerable excitement." On arrival at Grand Central Station, Dixon "resisted arrest." He was locked up at the Grand Central Police station and later bailed out by O'Rourke for $500. He appeared at the Yorkville police court to face charges for his behaviour on May 20.

The gruelling vaudeville travel and countless fights continued. Over the next year, Dixon defended his title nine times while still fighting exhibition bouts in his travelling show – Tommy Connelly in Boston, Mike Leonard in New York, Johnny Griffin back in Boston, Young Griffo and Frank Erne and Peddlar Palmer in New York, Jerry Marshall back in Boston, Kentucky Rosebud in Philadelphia, and Martin Flaherty in Boston. There were draws and wins and continued celebrations with drinking and gambling.

In late June of 1896, a physically and mentally exhausted Dixon announced he would take some time to relax through the summer and "appear in several important bouts in the fall."

A few days later, he announced a split with Tom O'Rourke. The *Boston Post* reported, "O'Rourke [was] far more incensed with George Dixon for jumping than he was with [his other notable boxer, Joe] Walcott." The cause for the split was never made clear. However, Dixon's spending was a point of increasing friction. O'Rourke tried unsuccessfully to keep Dixon on a budget. Dixon resisted. As well, one wonders if Dixon's carousing, and perhaps his womanizing, had caused too much strain with Kitty and by association with Tom O'Rourke. In either case, the split was traumatic for all involved.

The Boston Globe reported that Billy Madden was now in charge of George Dixon's affairs and would manage him, but by mid-August Dixon had split with him as well. "It appears," reported the Waterloo *Daily Courier*, "that there must have been something amiss in the camp of Billy Madden and George Dixon, for now Dixon denies that Billy is his manager and that he had any right to make any matches for him."

By that autumn, Tom O'Rourke and George Dixon – and perhaps by implication George and Kitty as well – had resolved their differences, at least temporarily. "In Boston," reported *The Boston Globe*, "it is believed that Tom O'Rourke and George Dixon will soon resume their old relations, Dixon having discovered that good managers are scarce."

A renewed Dixon, perhaps having made promises to O'Rourke about serious training, returned to fighting, engaging in as many as fifteen bouts a week. Most were still vaudeville exhibitions, but some were title defenses, coming as often as twice or three times a month.

Dixon's good behaviour, though, did not last long. Between bouts, his drinking was said to have worsened. "The little man began to step up his drinking," noted a reporter discussing the arc of Dixon's career after his fight with Jack Skelly in New Orleans in 1892, "carousing in the deadfalls of San Juan Hill, a seamier section of New York." Despite this, Dixon still managed to earn draws and wins against the best fighters in the game.

But it would not be long before he showed serious signs of weariness and weakness.

Round Eight

Right Hand Heart Blow: *The famous right hand heart blow is undoubtedly the most effective as well as the most dangerous of all body blows. I am writing this book during my leisure moments and evenings while training for my contest with Solly Smith of Los Angeles, California, which is to take place before the Coney Island Athletic Club on September 24, 1893, for a purse of ten thousand dollars. About eight weeks ago I saw Smith defeat Johnnie Griffen at Roby, Indiana, in very short order, and I realized the fact that I have the best man of my career to meet. He is a hard, quick puncher and takes excellent care of his jaw. By excellent care, I mean a good close guard. I have decided that the only way he can be whipped is by punching his body. If I can succeed in landing some clean body hits, I will soon cause him to lower his guard and then try for his jaw. The way I usually land a heart blow is by drawing my opponent on to lead with his left. As soon as he does, I cross guard my left arm in under his left, thus raising it up out of the way of a right hander under the heart.*

– George Dixon, "A Lesson in Boxing" (1893)

The growth of sports reporting in North American newspapers developed in tandem with the growth of modern boxing. In 1889, reports of boxing matches were regularly reported beneath the fold on page one of most papers. Yet as gambling became more prevalent in boxing and horse racing, and as baseball grew in popularity, a proto-sports page began to emerge. Chief among the newspapers that reported on sports, and chief among the newspapers that reported on boxing in particular, was the immensely popular and widely influential *Police Gazette*.

Founded in 1845 by journalist Enoch E. Camp and lawyer George Wilkes, the *Police Gazette* was originally created, in part, to publicize the building of the intercontinental railroad. Its name was chosen because the newspaper's other content focused on events and issues that were considered police matters – salacious crime, murders, outlaws, prostitution, and gambling – and by association the world of the "sport." The *Police Gazette* was tabloid in size and used numerous pictures – first ornate and detailed engravings and then photographs – as key components of its stories.

Images of scantily dressed dancers and strippers often pushed the limits of obscenity laws, but they also ensured a large and devoted readership. In the late nineteenth century, the *Police Gazette* became interested in boxing. Because no sanctioned organization existed to anoint champions, the paper became the unofficial organ to confer championship titles (until the newly formed National Boxing Association began to do so in 1920). This had much to do with its most famous editor.

Irish immigrant Richard Kyle Fox was the *Police Gazette*'s always passionate and often fiery editor during the heyday of the paper from 1878 until 1922. Before Fox's tenure, other newspapers routinely sent reporters to clandestine boxing matches – illegal in nearly all states – to report on the action. In an effort to have it both ways, these newspapers would report each fight in detail but then moralize against the sport. Fox had little time for such hypocrisy. From his first days at the paper, he used his boxing reports to encourage the sport's legalization and professionalization. He even promoted and sanctioned the fights. An astute newspaperman and businessman, Fox was not above creating public disputes in the pages of the *Police Gazette* to cultivate interest in a match. For instance, he long maintained a running dispute with John L. Sullivan, questioning Sullivan's skill in the ring, which did much to publicize both the sport and Sullivan's profile. As well, Fox promoted specific boxers. In 1890, Fox found in George Dixon a gentlemanly hero. Thereafter, he did much to promote Dixon's career and popularity.

* * *

In the barn of a New Jersey boxing hall, on November 26, 1896, George Dixon faced Frank Erne for the second time. Erne was a Swiss fighter who lived in Buffalo, New York. Five years younger than Dixon, Erne stood five feet six and weighed 121 pounds. He was quick and muscular with dark hair and piercing eyes, and he possessed an unusually long reach. Because Erne was above weight for an official featherweight bout, the outcome of the match would not affect Dixon's title.

The two men entered the ring at 10:00 p.m. when they were introduced by the referee to the more than four thousand fans. After the preliminaries, the bell rang at 10:05, and the fighters charged into the centre of the ring.

Probing each other for the opening seconds, Dixon struck first with a hard left hook to Erne's body. Erne countered with a right to Dixon's neck and then leaned back, jabbing with his left. Dixon threw a left to Erne's ear and another quick left to Erne's nose. But few punches had significant effect.

In the second round, the fighters stood close, exchanging punches and counterpunches. Dixon struck a right to Erne's ribs. Erne clinched and caught his breath. When they broke free, Erne delivered a blow to Dixon's mouth. And so it continued. At the end of the round, the referee scored the fight even, and the crowd's cheers grew as it became clear that Erne was a puzzle for which Dixon had no solution.

In the third, Erne took the lead with a right to Dixon's body, followed by a left to the head. Dixon rushed, forcing Erne to the ropes, and quickly turned the momentum. With Erne against the ropes, Dixon delivered an artful combination. Yet Erne was quick. He stepped out from the ropes and into the centre of the ring. Dixon turned and rushed again. Erne threw an overhand left that caught Dixon on the eye. Dixon again moved forward. Erne continued his retreating and counterattack. When the bell came, both fighters were raw with the best blows each could deliver.

In the fourth, Dixon was caught off guard by a left and was forced into the ropes. He changed tactics and bounded off the ropes with a surprise right that hit Erne on the jaw. Yet Erne stood fast and retaliated with a right hand of his own that cut Dixon above the left eye. Dixon countered. Erne pushed Dixon toward the corner. Dixon again bounded off the ropes, and the two boxers delivered blow and counterblow until they clinched and waited for the bell.

In the fifth and sixth rounds, Dixon struggled to connect with Erne's head, so he turned to the body, throwing right and left blows to the ribs. Erne waited and countered with strikes to Dixon's head. Dixon now eschewed the rush and counterpunch and focused a steady attack against Erne's body. Erne pushed Dixon toward the ropes and worked Dixon's increasingly swollen eyes.

Again and again the two stayed in close, exchanging hard blows. Blood flowed from Erne's nose. Then Dixon threw a right punch over Erne's heart. Erne returned with a combination left and right. By round eight, the intensity of the fight was wearing. Both fighters spent more time clinching, catching their breath, than they did punching. From then until round thirteen, the rhythm was set, with Dixon working on Erne's body, and Erne working at Dixon's eye. Both were exhausted.

In the fourteenth, Dixon began to falter. His stamina waned. The two fighters stood almost chin to chin, exchanging rights and lefts, clinching, breaking, and exchanging blows again. Erne found an opening and delivered a stinging right hand to Dixon's jaw. Dixon reeled. Erne rushed. Dixon fell back into the ropes with Erne delivering a flurry of blows. When the bell came, Dixon "looked worried as he sat down."

In the opening of the fifteenth round, Erne bolted from the stool. Dixon met him with a left hook. Erne easily countered, snapping Dixon's "head back with a heavy jab on the eye." Dixon could not get his balance and flailed. Erne connected again on Dixon's eye. Dixon was desperate and clinched. The crowed booed. In the sixteenth round, Erne continued to strike at Dixon, but he became careless, underestimating the champion.

Dixon blocked Erne's left and threw his own left to Erne's nose and a right to his ribs, where "the flesh had grown crimson from the blows that had landed there." Erne clinched and held on until the round's end. The seventeenth through nineteenth rounds continued in the same manner. The fight was conducted in close and the heavy exchanges were leaving their marks.

As the final round began, the two weary fighters shook hands and began again to exchange hard body blows. Erne hit Dixon with a left to the mouth. Dixon clinched and delivered a strike to Erne's stomach. The crowd, thinking the punch low, yelled, "Foul!" The referee ignored them. The two fighters again stood toe to toe, landing left and right combinations until the final bell sounded.

By all accounts, the fight had been a draw, so Dixon was stunned when the referee announced that Erne had won. The crowd of four thousand erupted in cheers. Erne leapt from his stool to hug his seconds. He then shot across the ring to Dixon, who shook his hand. Dixon "looked dejected" and stepped between the ropes to make his way to the dressing room.

The next day's papers seemed as one suggesting that the referee had it wrong and that the match was rightly a draw. Because of Erne's weight, Dixon maintained his championship – but only on a technicality. As the referee also noted, Dixon would "have to be beaten in a finish fight to lose his laurels." The loss only made clear to all that Dixon was now vulnerable. Eleven months later, he would see just how vulnerable.

"When George Dixon loses his featherweight title as he some day must," wrote New York's *The Sun*, "he couldn't shed the crown more gracefully than in such a contest as that of last night [against Erne] – beyond the odds, the greatest featherweight battle the eyes have ever seen. He cut out the pace for himself as cycle racing people say, and did things so well as to be uncanny."

* * *

In late December 1896, Frank Erne, recognizing the worth of a rematch, immediately negotiated for another with Dixon. "Dixon don't appear to be satisfied with the whipping that I gave him," Erne said, goading Dixon, "so to set all doubts at rest, my manager has decided that the proper course to pursue is to give him a chance to retrieve his lost laurels and at the same time enable me to prove conclusively that I am the featherweight champion. If Dixon is my superior, here is a chance to prove it before the club offering the best inducements."

But before a rematch could be set with Frank Erne, Dixon returned to the ring with others, beating Torpedo Billy Murphy and drawing with Jack Downey in January and February of 1897.

Dixon met Frank Erne again in March of 1897 in front of six thousand spectators. Erne had swelled to 130 pounds, but Dixon was anxious to prove his mettle. They met at the Broadway Athletic club. "Dixon was himself again," noted a *New York Times* reporter, "leading the fight through the twenty-first round." Erne seemed unable to land any effective blows. The fight was notable for Dixon's change in fighting style, showing a more careful and cautious approach.

He took the decision in twenty-five rounds.

* * *

In April 1897, he beat Johnny Griffin in twenty rounds and drew fights with Kentucky Rosebud in Philadelphia and Dal Hawkins in California in June and July, before meeting Solly Smith in Woodward's Pavilion in San Francisco on October 4, 1897.

The two had met before, of course, in September of 1893, at the Coney Island Athletic Club, where Tom O'Rourke guaranteed Smith $8,000 if he won and $1,000 if he lost. Dixon had won decisively then, in a seventh round knockout. As such, as Dixon and O'Rourke made their way to San Francisco for the next Smith fight, the betting for the rematch was nearly two to one for Dixon.

At the fight, the local press in California noted that all social classes were represented in the large crowd. George Dixon entered the ring at 9:15 p.m. with Tom O'Rourke, Young Mitchell, and "Scaldy Bill" Quinn, who was "attired in a turtle-neck sweater and a wheelman's cap." Solly Smith followed Dixon, accompanied by Spider Kelly, Tom Lansing, and Tom McGrath. Though Dixon heard much support from the "Afro-Americans" in attendance, it was Smith who received the loudest cheers.

The San Francisco Call noted that Dixon, "the little colored featherweight wonder," has "seen his best days." Although "he still retains his old-time cleverness," he is now "lacking in precision and driving power." It is difficult to know if the paper was expressing a genuine, clear-eyed assessment of Dixon, or whether it was engaging in the sort of subtle racism that was endemic in such reporting.

When referee George Green finished, and the bell finally sounded opening round one, both fighters stepped quickly to the centre of the ring. Smith threw a left that caught Dixon on the nose, followed by another to his jaw. Surprised by Smith's speed, Dixon clinched. When they broke, Dixon swung twice at Smith but only glanced his arms. Smith countered with a shot to Dixon's head. Again Dixon clinched.

In round two, Dixon rushed forward but was still unable to land any blows. Smith just sidestepped and landed a left to Dixon's nose. Dixon countered, catching Smith in the ribs. Smith blocked Dixon's follow-up to his head and returned with a sound shot to Dixon's jaw. At the bell, the referee scored the fight even.

In round three, both fighters connected effectively with their blows. Dixon caught Smith with a right uppercut to the jaw. Smith missed with a left. Dixon struck with another left to Smith's jaw. Smith was stunned. Dixon stepped in closer and delivered a combination to Smith's body. Smith took the blows and recovered his balance. The two settled into cautious exchanges for the middle minute. Both fighters then rushed forward. Smith missed with his right, while Dixon connected with a left in Smith's ribs. Smith threw a right uppercut that connected with Dixon's head. Then the two offered little more than probing punches. The round ended even.

A contemporary drawing of the fight shows Dixon leaning back and blocking a hard right from Smith. The referee is not shown, but the fighters' seconds are there, kneeling in the corners with anxious looks on their faces. Around the ring, hundreds of spectators cheer and jeer and gamble.

For the next twelve rounds, the two fighters continued to strike and counterstrike. In the final five rounds, Smith began to accrue points by evading Dixon's combinations and connecting with sound blows. In the final round, the fighters approached each other, smiled, and shook hands, acknowledging the hard-fought battle. The round continued as the others had, with well-placed blows and effective defenses. When the bell finally rang, both exhausted combatants returned to their corners. The referee hesitated only briefly before he pointed to Smith and announced that he was the winner. The crowd cheered, while among the "Afro-Americans" assembled "a wail arose."

Dixon had lost his featherweight title.

* * *

After the fight, reporters from *The San Francisco Call* spoke with both fighters. "Yes," Smith said, "I did the trick as I expected. In my first fight with Dixon, I was too confident and grew careless, so I made up my mind to take no chances this time. At no time in the fight was I at all tired, and as you can see I haven't got a mark on me; the amount of it is he couldn't land at all. I hurt my right hand in the eighth or ninth round, and therefore didn't use it as often as I otherwise should."

Dixon was disappointed. "Well," he said, "I can't be winning all the time; though to give the fight to Smith I don't think was a fair decision. I am just as fresh now as I was at any time during the fight. No, those body punches didn't hurt me, as I blocked most of them. Anyway, I guess I won't have to beg for a living. There's plenty of fight in me yet."

The news of Dixon's defeat was greeted throughout California with great enthusiasm. In Sacramento, each round was reported by a representative of *The San Francisco Call* via Western Union Telegraphs, "at the clubrooms of the Golden Eagle Hotel." The barroom, billiard room, and hotel lobby, reported the paper, were packed to overflowing. Between rounds, the patrons loudly discussed the "merits of the two contestants." When the caller's voice announced a new round had begun, the "silence [was] so intense that the proverbial pin would have been heard had it dropped."

In Stockton, California, hundreds of interested people gathered on Main Street to hear the bulletins read by the Western Union agent, "and to study them afterward as they [were] tacked up on the bulletin board." It was said that "half the colored population [was] out, anxious to hear" about the fight. In Los Angeles, the interest in the fight was compared to that of the last "national election." A crowd of more than a thousand stood on Spring Street to see the bulletins "thrown by stereopticon upon a large screen, and cheered as the news was pleasing to friends of either combatant."

Similar scenes were played out in Chico, Oakland, Woodland, and at Marysville, California, where there was a "surging mass eager to read the bulletins posted on the spacious show window" of Buttleman's cigar store.

There were many who believed the referee's decision was wrong. "There can be no doubt," said one disgruntled California sport, "that it was a put-up job, but I think there were only three or four on the inside. My opinion is that O'Rourke instructed Dixon to go in and fight and refrain from knocking the Los Angeles boy out. He knew that if Smith stayed the twenty rounds, he would get the decision because [referee] George Green has had it in for the colored bruiser ever since he went up against Joe Walcott and got the worst of it. After giving Dixon his instructions, I think O'Rourke, Dixon, and a couple of others backed Solly heavily and that they are a few hundreds better off today. One thing that strengthens this belief in me is the way O'Rourke is talking about being robbed. I believe he is talking for effect. I have known O'Rourke for years, and he is one of the gamest losers I ever saw, even when he knows he is being jobbed. If the men fight again, I will stake every cent I can raise on Dixon winning. I want to see them fight to a finish."

The reporter who quoted this sport had his own doubts. However, he did grant that Dixon might win the next meeting of the two. "George Dixon," he wrote in the *Oakland Tribune*, "has been one of the greatest fighters that ever lived. I believe his record will never be equaled, but he has retrograded and has met a man who outclasses him in every way, even as Smith will meet his superior if he stays long enough in the business.

George Dixon is not the man he was a few years ago, nor can he ever hope to be again."

Two months later, in December, Tom O'Rourke announced that Dixon would stop fighting and rest until he met Solly Smith again in February.

* * *

Meantime, in Macon, Georgia, Oscar Williams was riding a train to Atlanta. The young black man had been charged with an assault on the daughter of a Henry County farmer, and the local police were worried about his safety in the Macon jail. The train had left Macon at 4:20, and all was well until the train was forty miles from Atlanta. At the town of Griffin, a mob of armed men boarded the train. When they found the shocked Williams, they dragged him from the train and through the main street, where locals were heard to cheer. About two hundred yards outside the town limits, the mob gathered round a large tree. A rope was tied to a lower branch and Williams was hanged. Afterward, his body was riddled with more than five hundred bullets.

No one was charged with the killing.

Round Nine

Pivot Blow: *The 'pivot blow' derives its name from the fact that you turn or pivot in order to deliver it. This is the blow with which George La Blanche, the Marine, gave grave Jack Dempsey his first defeat. Previous to that noted battle, the pivot blow was almost unheard of, and since then, it has been barred by nearly all the big athletic clubs where boxing matches are held. Some persons claim it a foul blow, but such is not so, as a man can land a pivot blow with his hand without striking his opponent with his elbow. To land a 'pivot' blow wait until your opponent leads with his left at your face. Then place your left arm against the outer side of his left arm and hold it firm. The instant the arms meet raise your right foot, the force of your opponent's arm coming against your arm will spin the body around with much force. Judge as nearly as possible the distance of your opponent's head and aim the blow for the point of the jaw. The odds are against your landing it, but if it does, you will find it a very effective punch.*

– George Dixon, "A Lesson in Boxing" (1893)

On March 17, 1898, the Syracuse *Evening Herald* reported that Dixon had injured himself. "While training early this week," reported the paper, "George Dixon, who was scheduled to meet Tommy White next Monday evening, slipped and wrenched his right ankle. The ankle continued swelling and last night Tom O'Rourke was compelled to wire the Empire Athletic Club asking for a postponement. This is the first time since he has been in the fighting business that Dixon has ever had to ask for a postponement, and he feels badly about it."

* * *

On July 4, 1898, Dixon was hosting a party with friends at his home in Malden, Massachusetts. With him was fellow boxer and future champion welterweight Joe Walcott. As the group prepared fireworks to celebrate the holiday, Walcott lit a large firecracker and, while swinging it above his head "after the manner of a candle," it exploded. He was taken to the hospital where surgery was performed on his hand. Though he spent months rehabilitating his hand, Walcott recovered.

* * *

As Dixon's drinking and gambling worsened, O'Rourke seemed unable to keep Dixon's finances in order. Dixon's debts grew and, as a consequence, he lost possessions. "Dixon owns a small wooden dwelling house out in Faulkner Street, Malden," reported *The Boston Globe*, "saved from the wreck of a fortune." Likely, this house was different from the large house he had owned with Kitty. Certainly, Kitty must have found the change of fortune difficult, and her love for George must have been sorely tested. Though no record exists that speaks to their deteriorating relationship, it seems clear that George and Kitty were growing apart.

In late July 1898, John L. Sullivan spoke about George Dixon with a reporter of the *Evening Times* and alluded to his recent setbacks. "As a rule," said the ever irascible Sullivan, "I have no use for colored people and never would fight a colored man. But Dixon is the greatest little man I ever saw, and there will never be another like him. He has tackled lightweights, welterweights, and people bigger than himself, but not one of them has been able to put him out. He ought to quit, for like myself, he is a 'has been.'"

Sullivan then left Boston for St. Louis, where he was scheduled to umpire a ball game.

* * *

On August 10, 1898, two hundred men surrounded the jailhouse in Clarendon, Arkansas, demanding the jailer hand over four black prisoners, three men and one woman – Will Sanders, Rilla Weaver, Dennis Record, and Manse Castle – who had all been charged with murder. The jailer, R.F. Milwee, had only a second officer with him. From behind the locked door, Milwee told the crowd that there were twenty-five men with him, and that they would fire on anyone who tried to enter. Many among the mob hesitated, and they talked among themselves for a time. But in the end, they rushed forward and forced the door.

Inside, Milwee thought better of resisting and handed over the cell keys. The four prisoners were dragged from their cells outside to the elevated tramway of a sawmill just a hundred yards behind the jailhouse. They were hanged there, and their bodies remained until 9:00

the next morning. By then, great crowds had come to view the "gruesome sight" of the bodies, hanging six feet from the ground "with tongues protruding and ropes cutting deep into their necks."

No one was charged with the murders.

* * *

On September 21, 1898, the *Halifax Herald* in Dixon's hometown ran an article about its native son. "The Halifax Pugilist Squandered $200,000 in Ten Years on Horses, Gambling, and Friends" ran the headline.

"Getting rid of over $200,000 has not apparently impaired his health or weakened his physical abilities," noted the paper. "Dixon is today in active life and holds the same position he did when gold or its equivalent rolled in upon him by the thousand. His weakness has been the horses. He liked to take a chance on the racetracks. He evidently found very few sure tips for his ledger carries no profits providing his expertness as a betting man. He had other weaknesses to help him scatter his money. He has had his virtues. Many an orphan and widow have cause to remember his charity. They have shared with him his hard-earned money. This spendthrift enjoys two-fold notoriety. He is colored and is a world-beater among his people in this ability to earn and spend money.

"He is a world beater in another way also, for his is no less than the featherweight champion of the world. George Dixon is yet to find a man of his weight who can stand before him in the ring and be there still standing in a contest to a finish. Of course that has meant that purse after purse has come to his pockets, thousands after thousands have been won by the vigor of his heart, sturdiness of his legs, and the strength of his long arms. If the money he had earned had gone to a bank or he had purchased real estate, he would to-day be classed among the richest colored men in the world.

"He liked to bet on the horses. He liked to pass a social evening with the sporting men the world over. His heart made him open to all pleas of charity, especially for the aid of the members of his own race. He has but few dollars to-day, and when the first defeat comes, as it must come to him as it does to everybody else, he may have to hustle for the dollar that will be necessary to keep himself and his white wife.

"He began fighting anybody and everybody for purses from $25 to $75. He continued by winning stakes amounting to $12,500. Beginning as a boy in the Boston photograph gallery of Elmer Chickering at a small salary, Dixon jumped into the front rank of pugilists at a bound. His first big fight in a financial sense was with Gene Hornbacker. Dixon won with consummate ease, and put in his pocket something like $750. Then followed his memorable 70-round draw with Cal McCarthy in this city, the incentive being a purse of a thousand dollars.

"During the year 1890, Dixon visited England, defeating Nunc Wallace, winning $2,000 and a large amount of outside betting by touring through the United Kingdom giving sparring exhibitions. He cleared nearly $9,000. On his return he defeated Johnny Murphy and picked up something like $3,000. During the remainder of that year he toured with a theatrical company and earned an average of from $300 to $5,000. During 1891, George defeated Cal McCarthy, winning $3,280 and made an easy victim of Abe Willis, getting therefore $4,500 besides some large bets. Besides this, he performed in theatres all over the country and a conservative estimate of his winnings that year places them in the neighborhood of $16,000."

Why the paper chose to focus so intently on Dixon's finances is unclear, though the paper would know the dark fascination with a successful person's fall is always of public interest.

* * *

On November 11, 1898, George Dixon met Dave Sullivan at the Lenox Athletic Club in New York City. Sullivan was an Irish boxer from Boston, five feet four and seven years younger than Dixon. He had black hair and brown eyes, which always expressed a look of fierce determination. In September 1898, Sullivan had beaten Solly Smith in five rounds for the featherweight title. The fight was lopsided and had to be stopped in the fifth. During the second round, Smith had broken his arm, near the wrist. But he fought on for three more rounds, until it became clear that he could continue no more. In this way, Sullivan had become the unlikely featherweight champion.

On the day of his fight with Dixon, Sullivan was more than a pound overweight. The weigh-in referee gave him an hour to drop the weight. For most of that time, he ran through the streets of New York. When he returned and was weighed again, he had dropped the pound. He then raced to his dressing room to prepare for the fight.

Referee Jimmy Colville was waiting in the ring as Dixon entered first and took the southwest corner. The crowd grew restless as they waited for Sullivan, who arrived more than fifteen minutes late. The fighters shed their robes and then took instructions from the referee. Both fighters, it was clear to all, looked fit and focused.

At 10:32 p.m., the bell rang for round one. Cautious in the first minute, both fighters danced and circled, until Sullivan caught Dixon in the ribs. Dixon clinched, broke away, and delivered a combination to Sullivan's head. In the second round, Dixon landed a stiff left on Sullivan's jaw, which Sullivan countered gamely, offering a combination to Dixon's ribs. Dixon defended well. They exchanged hard blows left and right. In the third round, both delivered explosive punches, though Sullivan got the worst of it. For the next seven rounds, Dixon grew stronger, while Sullivan's intensity and accuracy waned.

In the tenth round, Dixon drove a left into Sullivan's jaw.

Sullivan dropped.

Shaking his head, he slowly climbed back to his feet only to receive two quick blows. All Sullivan could do was clinch and shake off the assault. But Dixon broke away and hit Sullivan with a left so hard that Sullivan buckled and slipped between the ropes. Sullivan rose, returned to the ring, and after he was checked by the referee, offered only a feeble defense against Dixon's relentless assault. Finally, Sullivan's brother climbed into the ring to stop the fight, but a nearby policeman called him out. So Dixon continued his attack. Sullivan, exhausted and dazed, dropped his hands, helpless.

The referee stopped the fight.

After some argument with Sullivan's seconds, referee Colville awarded the fight, and the featherweight title, to George Dixon. He had become the first boxer in history to lose and regain a title.

A revived Dixon went on to win ten of eleven defenses of his newly regained title, the other fight being a draw. It seemed Dixon had recaptured something of his old self.

* * *

In early February of 1899, the New York *Sun* published a review of Dixon's career following his knockout of a twenty-eight-year-old black fighter named Young Pluto in New York in front of five thousand spectators. Born in Saint John, New Brunswick, Pluto called Perth, Australia, home. Before fighting Dixon, Pluto had only lost two fights in thirty-eight. But Dixon proved too much for him.

"That Dixon boy is the most wonderful fighter in the world," read *The Sun*'s headline. "Modest and unassuming, Dixon had just shaken hands with his defeated foe and was hurrying out of the ring as if anxious to get out of the public gaze. There was no proud stalking, no grandstand business about him, such as other champion fighters like to indulge in, but he simply followed out his old habit of taking his victory with indifference. There is no better-behaved fighter in the country than the little colored man, who has probably fought more battles than anyone else. Tom O'Rourke, his manager, says that Dixon's sole ambition is to fight rather than to gain notoriety by means of newspaper talk. He has never yet refused to meet a challenger and has always been ready to agree upon any rules to govern the contest. Dixon's methods in the ring have also placed him above reproach. He believes in fair fighting, adhering strictly to the rules and the instructions of the referee. What few decisions have been rendered against him failed to arouse the champion's ire, for he always looks upon a referee as honest. In a word, Dixon tries to be a gentleman and a sportsman at all times. Those who have received verdicts over him are George Wright, Billy Plimmer, Frank Erne, Solly Smith and Ben Jordan, all in limited round bouts."

The reporter from *The Sun* chatted amiably with Dixon after his victory over Pluto. Dixon was lying on a table with his seconds rubbing him down.

"How many fights have you been involved in, George?" asked the reporter.

"I have fought about 100 limited round bouts since I first came into prominence in 1888," said George, "and I have also taken part in 700 four-round contests, meeting all comers on the road." He smiled. "That's quite a record, isn't it?"

The reporter smiled back and nodded. "In all that time, how many times have you been knocked down?"

"Only once," said Dixon, "and that was in a three-round exhibition bout with the 'Kentucky Rosebud' in Philadelphia several years ago. I got out of a sickbed to meet the engagement, and in the second round, 'Rosebud' saw a chance to gain some fame. We were boxing lightly, per agreement, when suddenly he sneaked in a punch on my jaw, which sent me to the floor like a log. When I got up the 'Rosebud' ran about the ring until the bout was over. That was the only time I lost my legs."

The reporter scribbled Dixon's response in his notebook. When he finished, he asked, "How did you happen to get into pugilism?"

"I was always fond of scrapping and one day while mixing it up with a fellow bigger than myself in a little club in Boston, Tom O'Rourke, my manager, discovered me. I held my own pretty well on that occasion and O'Rourke asked me if I wanted to be a champion. I said yes, of course, but I had no idea I ever would be. Eugene Hornbacker was a crack featherweight then and O'Rourke brought me to New York to make a match. I beat this man very quickly and then set sail for the champion, Cal McCarthy. We were matched to fight to a finish on January 7, 1890, and the battle took place in a little hall over a bank in Washington Street, Boston. I weighted 103 pounds, and the fight lasted all night. At the end of the seventieth round, the referee called it a draw."

Dixon rolled over on the table, adjusted his towel, and continued.

"In 1891, I tackled McCarthy again, in Troy," Dixon said, "and beat him well in twenty-two rounds, although I had him out in the third. Madden and McAuliffe jumped into the ring at that period, but the referee ordered the fight to proceed. I weighted 107 pounds and was in great shape. During the fight I broke my little finger, which was the only time I ever hurt my hands. That victory gave me the championship."

"What was the hardest battle you ever fought?" asked the reporter.

"With Young Griffo, at Coney Island," answered Dixon. "It was a twenty-five round bout. Griffo weighed 147 pounds and I scaled at 122, the featherweight limit [at the time]. I found the Australian was a wonderful boxer, more scientific, in fact, than anybody I ever met before or since. It was a fast fight and one of the best on record to look at, I believe."

The reporter nodded, made a few more notes. "How many times have opponents marked your face?"

Dixon smiled. "Solly Smith made me bleed quite a lot when we met at Coney Island some years ago, but that did not prevent me from knocking him out. Erne, Tommy White and several others also succeeded in making the claret flow, but that is nothing if a fellow is sound in body, limb, and wind."

"What are the lowest and highest weights at which you have fought?"

"The lowest was 103 pounds," answered Dixon, "and the highest, 124. I am lighter now than for some time past. When I began training for the 'Pluto' fight, I weighted 109½ pounds, but I soon built myself up to 119. Then I worked to 115, at which weight I entered the ring. Yet I am just as strong as I would be if I weighted 124."

"Who is the best featherweight in this country," asked the reporter, "barring yourself?" He smiled.

"I think [Oscar] Gardner is the man," said Dixon. "I've met him in a twenty-five round bout and know what he can do. Some day he may succeed me as champion, for he is improving steadily and is a powerful hitter. Ben Jordan, the English Champion, who got a decision over me, is also a splendid featherweight, but I think I can beat him if we ever meet again."

The reporter turned the notebook sheet and continued writing. "Do you prefer limited-round bouts to finish fights?" he asked.

"I have no preference," said Dixon. "Finish fights decide beyond a doubt who is the better man, while sometimes there is a difference of opinion when a limited-round bout ends. But finish contests appear to be out of date nowadays."

The reporter asked a few more questions and then thanked Dixon. When he returned to his office, he concluded his article with some observations: "Dixon says he will be 29 years old next July. He has been married for ten years. In training for fights he generally conducts his own work, as he knows from experience how to get fit. He is a hard worker and is conscientious to a fault. He says O'Rourke, as his second, has been of inestimable service to him. Some day Dixon will be summarily beaten, as nearly all pugilists are, but he will always be remembered as a phenomenal fighter and a square little man."

* * *

Dixon returned to the ring five times over the next two months, defeating Kid Broad in Buffalo, Joe Bernstein in Brooklyn, Sam Bolen in Louisville, Tommy White in Denver, and Eddie Santry in Chicago. In August of 1899, Dixon fought Eddie Santry again in New York. Though his fights were victories, Dixon's performances in the ring were growing inconsistent. In his second fight with Eddie Santry, the *Republican News* of Ohio reported that "Dixon at times was wild, and he frequently overreached himself, using poor judgment as to distance."

In October and November 1899, Dixon fought and beat Tim Callahan, Will Curley, and Eddie Lenny as he prepared for a much anticipated fight with Terry McGovern. In these fights, he fought well, but something seemed amiss. His speed had lessened and his combinations were not as sharp. Whether he was consciously aware of any changes in his own fighting is unclear.

But it was clear that Dixon was looking to his future after boxing. He began preparing for a graceful exit from the ring as champion. In late November 1899, "prominent eastern sporting men" arranged a "monster benefit" for George Dixon "to commemorate the colored champion's retirement from the ring." The benefit was set for two weeks following his fight with Terry McGovern.

"There is a period in the career of every fighting man when it is time to quit," reported *The Boston Globe*, "and George Dixon, the cleverest, toughest, and most industrious of the workers in his class, feels he has reached that point ... He has decided that his battle with Terry McGovern shall be the last fight for him. Dixon has been in the ring continuously for more than thirteen years and for nine years he has held the championship of his class. He is, without question, the greatest fighter that his race has ever produced."

Perhaps reflecting his recent lacklustre fights, Dixon's once invincible reputation gave way to doubts among gamblers. Days before the fight with Terry McGovern the *Newark Advocate* reported, "McGovern is now pronounced the favorite in the betting." McGovern was, the paper added, "much younger than Dixon, and this no doubt has influenced the bettors." Tom O'Rourke still had great confidence in his fighter, betting $1,500 at even odds on Dixon to win in ten rounds.

Never shy about offering his opinions, John L. Sullivan weighed in on Dixon's prospects. "I am afraid Little Chocolate is up against it," Sullivan told *The Daily Northwestern*, "and I confess that I hate to see him whipped. This Brooklyn lad [McGovern] is as good as Dixon when Dixon was at his best, and perhaps he is better. No one has tried him out lately, and I doubt if Dixon will be able to give him a tryout. McGovern will win because he can hit three times as hard as any boy of his pounds in the ring today, and he can hit even harder than most of the lightweights. He doesn't have to set or steady himself to slug. He can slug from an angle, hit going or coming, on his heels or on his toes. If ever a fighter was born to make trouble for his fellow men with the gloves his name is Terry McGovern, and I'm glad to hear that he has enough horse sense to take care of himself and save his money."

In the November 16, 1899, edition of the *Evening Telegraph*, Dixon again announced that he would retire from fighting after the McGovern fight, regardless of the outcome. The *Evening Telegraph* said of Dixon, he had "a clean, reputable and valiant career. There is no question but that he has been the best fighter in his class, since he won the world's championship, and he has fought more times than any man that ever graced the ring." The paper also reported that Dixon intended to retire to

New York and open a "saloon business with a popular colored jockey."

On December 29, 1899, Sullivan responded to boxing writer Ben Benton who had asked his opinion on the coming fight. "My Dear Benton," wrote Sullivan in a brief letter, "you can state that McGovern will beat Dixon sure and inside of 10 rounds. That is as sure as your name is Ben Benton. Take my tip for that. Although Dixon is a great little colored boy, this is the time he will meet his Waterloo, although it will be no credit to any one who does defeat him because he has gone a fast slip like myself. But never mind that. McGovern could beat him in his best day and I do not want you to think I am prejudiced. I am far from being such. Yours truly, John L. Sullivan."

* * *

On the evening of the fight, January 9, 1900, the air in the Broadway Athletic Club was thick with cigar smoke and the rumble of an excited crowd. The two fighters made their way into the ring amid hearty cheers. Referee Johnny White called them to the centre and explained the rules. Then Dixon and McGovern shook hands and returned to their corners.

At the bell, the fighters sparred with caution, each waiting for an opening. McGovern struck first, catching Dixon with a left to his eye. Dixon responded in kind. They clinched, and when they broke, Dixon unloaded a hard left to McGovern's nose. McGovern staggered back. Dixon followed and delivered a combination of punches to McGovern's chest. After cautious sparring, the round went to Dixon.

McGovern adjusted his approach for round two. When Dixon threw a sharp left, McGovern ducked, stepped in, and shot Dixon hard in the ribs. Dixon countered with two lefts to McGovern's stomach. They stayed in close, exchanging blows. Dixon struck McGovern in the head with a straight right. McGovern fell halfway through the ropes. Dixon pursued, throwing a solid left hook to the neck. McGovern recovered his balance but staggered about the ring. The crowd roared at Dixon's assault. At the bell, Dixon had round two.

Round three saw the fighters in close, Dixon hooking a right to McGovern's jaw, and McGovern countering with a right to Dixon's body. Dixon threw a combination to the stomach and mouth, stunning McGovern, who countered with two missed blows. Then Dixon delivered unanswered lefts to McGovern's face. McGovern managed a weak response with a right to Dixon's jaw. Round three went to Dixon.

In the fourth, the floor betting moved to even on Dixon. In the ring, the fighters clinched. Dixon twice shot McGovern in the jaw. McGovern wobbled. Then he surprised Dixon with a right to the jaw. Dixon staggered. McGovern took the charge and shot a right hand to Dixon's heart and two quick jabs to the neck. Dixon fell against the ropes. McGovern moved in. Dixon clinched. McGovern let loose a hard right to the jaw. Dixon slumped as the bell rang. Round four to McGovern.

In the fifth round, both fighters threw heavy combinations, McGovern finding Dixon's jaw, Dixon finding McGovern's eye and stomach. McGovern focused on Dixon's ribs. He swung hard, but missed and fell to the canvas. As he rose, Dixon delivered a sharp combination to his head. McGovern recovered and countered with combinations to the ribs and heart.

In the sixth round, McGovern continued his assault on the body, with a hard left to Dixon's stomach. The fighters clinched. They broke. McGovern turned his attention to Dixon's head, throwing two hard blows. Dixon connected with his left to McGovern's head. They danced. McGovern switched to Dixon's stomach and then he delivered a left to Dixon's mouth that drew blood. They clinched at the bell.

In the seventh round, the fighters stood toe to toe and exchanged punches to the head and heart. McGovern struck at Dixon's stomach and offered a combination that pushed Dixon back to the ropes. In the eighth, Dixon struck McGovern in the neck, while McGovern shot at Dixon's stomach. In a clinch that followed, Dixon was thrown to the floor. When he rose, McGovern delivered two devastating blows to Dixon's stomach. Dixon dropped hard to the canvas, struggling to breathe. McGovern helped Dixon up, but Dixon looked winded and tired and threw himself into a clinch. McGovern pushed away and delivered a devastating right to the head.

Dixon dropped to the canvas.

Tom O'Rourke could take no more. He reached into the corner bucket and threw the sponge into the ring. The fight was over.

Dixon had lost his title again.

* * *

Following the fight, Dixon confirmed his intentions to retire. He returned home to Kitty and spent days in his Malden home contemplating his future. Despite his return, his relationship with Kitty was tense. The years of travelling, gambling, and drinking – and by strong suggestion, carousing with other women – had their effect on her. Yet, out of love or loyalty, she had stood by him. Ultimately, George would leave Kitty. And whether Kitty divorced George is uncertain. But by 1900, what remained of their relationship were just shadows and memory.

* * *

In February of 1900, the planned fundraiser was held in honour of Dixon's retirement. Present were champions and former champions – Terry McGovern, Jim Corbett, Tom Sharkey, Frank Erne, Joe Choynski, Joe Gans, and others – who agreed to put on fundraising exhibitions. Ticket sales brought in nearly $8,000. After a few playful bouts among the champions, George Dixon and Terry McGovern entered the ring themselves for a three-round exhibition. The two shook hands and McGovern presented Dixon with a $500 check. The crowd applauded and Dixon then thanked all who had contributed to his benefit and thanked "his fellow fighters for their kindness."

Then, as John L. Sullivan had done after his loss to Jim Corbett, Dixon looked to McGovern and then the audience and said he was glad that "when I met my Waterloo, it was handed to me by an American."

Following his retirement benefit, Dixon decided to enter the saloon business. "Never again will George Dixon, the retired colored featherweight of marvelous record, administer knock-out drops with five-ounce gloves," reported *The Daily Northwestern*, on March 20, 1900. "Instead, he will ladle out the sleep-producing potions with five-ounce glasses. He has purchased the café at 511 Sixth Avenue, New York."

It was soon clear that Dixon was no businessman and that the settled life would not sit well. He gave up on retirement and sold his saloon to lightweight fighter and friend Joe Gans. Said Dixon, "The humdrum business life does not agree with me." In April 1900, just two months after retiring, he announced he would fight again.

Tom O'Rourke would be his manager, he said, and he would take on Benny Yanger on June 5. "Now, it may be that not vanity, but the pinch of want forces Dixon back into the ring, and it is bread, not glory, that he is looking for," reported *The Daily Northwestern*, in April 1900. "If so, all the more's the pity, for in his day Dixon made a great deal of money, and was always known as a very square, good-hearted fellow."

Round Ten

Guard For Pivot Blow: *There are many different ways in which the 'pivot' blow can be avoided. For instance, by jumping back, by ducking the head or stepping to the left of your opponent while he is turning around to deliver the blow. Cut No. 10 shows a guard for the 'pivot' blow as well as giving you a chance to land a counter blow. To accomplish this guard, raise your right forearm in a perpendicular manner and the blow being of a swinging nature is bound to come against the arm in the same manner as shown in the accompanying cut. As soon as your right arm meets your opponent's right arm, strike out with your left hand for the body, and unless he is an exceptionally quick fellow in getting away, you will have landed a straight left hand blow under or near the heart. Take good care not to drop your right forearm guard as your opponent may try to land what is known as a 'shifting' blow with his left hand. The 'shifting' blow is the most effective left hand blow that is known.*

— George Dixon, "A Lesson in Boxing" (1893)

Unable to find a rewarding life after boxing, and likely unable to keep money in his pocket, Dixon returned to the ring and began a long, slow decline. He fought Tim Callahan in June 1900, losing in eight rounds. Then he drew with Benny Yanger in an uninspiring six rounds. He fought Terry McGovern again in late July, losing in six rounds.

A week later he fought Tommy Sullivan in Brooklyn. Reported the *Durango Democrat*, "'The one time invincible Dixon succumbed to Tommy Sullivan, of Brooklyn, at Coney Island tonight. The end came as the men shaped up for the seventh round, when Tom O'Rourke admitted defeat for his man, and claiming his left arm was disabled, refused to permit him to continue. Dixon was getting the worst of it. Sullivan was willing to mix it up on the slightest provocation and the consensus of opinion was that Dixon was well beaten." O'Rourke knew Dixon was no longer up for the challenge, and the two parted company.

Dixon felt betrayed.

In February 1901, Dixon accepted a fight with Harry Lyons, who was five inches taller and nearly ten pounds heavier than Dixon. When asked by a reporter, Tom O'Rourke said George was "unfit" to enter the ring. An anonymous letter sent to Baltimore Police Chief Hamilton indicated that Dixon was "in bad physical condition and that serious results might occur should he receive a 'rib-roaster' or solar plexus blow." Though never implicated, O'Rourke may well have written the letter.

On the night before the fight, Chief Hamilton and Deputy Farnan asked Dixon to report to the police station for an examination. Dixon arrived and stripped for the officers. Dixon smiled. "Give me a thump in the ribs," he said to the chief, "and see if you make me grunt." The chief did not smile. He just shook his head and pronounced Dixon fit to fight.

The match surprised most, as Dixon gave as good as he got, earning a draw after the scheduled eight rounds. "The entire bout was very pretty from a scientific standpoint," reported *The Boston Globe*. "Dixon deserved the credit on account of the handicap of meeting a bigger and stronger adversary."

In the spring of 1901, Dixon travelled alone to Colorado, to Ryan's Sand Creek training camp where future heavyweight champion Jack Johnson, who was in attendance, would describe the fighters as "a motley crew of scrappers." Indeed, the best boxers in world passed through – heavyweights Jack Johnson, Tom Sharkey, Bob Armstrong, and "Mexican Pete" Everett; welterweight "New York" Jack O'Brien; and featherweights Abe Attell, Young Corbett II, and George Dixon. Also present were trainers Spider Kelly and Tommy Ryan. The young Jack Johnson remembered it as an outstanding gathering of gifted fighters who spent their days trading punches and nights trading stories.

On August 16, 1901, Dixon fought Young Corbett II in Denver. He had again promised to retire from the ring if he lost. But when he lost, he kept on fighting. A week later, with Jack Johnson acting as his second, Dixon fought the gifted Abe Attell to a ten-round draw. Johnson later claimed he earned $150 on the fight and doubled it gambling.

In September 1901, Dixon travelled to Missouri to fight Benny Yanger, losing in fifteen rounds. In October, he fought Abe Attell twice more, first in Cripple Creek and then in Saint Louis, in front of sellout crowds. "The milling was tame throughout, the blows of both principals lacking steam," reported *The Boston Globe* about the second Attell fight. "There was a great deal of clinching in every round. The decision was displeasing to the majority of the spectators, who were of the opinion that Dixon was entitled to a draw at least."

In early December, Dixon announced he would take a rest for several months. "He surely deserves one," commented *The Boston Globe*. But by mid-December 1901, Dixon was back in the ring, losing to Austin Rice in Connecticut, drawing with Joe Tipman in Maryland, and losing to Eddie Lenny in Baltimore. For the next five months, Dixon travelled north and east, fighting lesser and lesser boxers and earning smaller and smaller purses: a win against Chick Tucker in Connecticut, a draw against Billy Ryan in Ottawa, Ontario, another draw against Danny Dougherty in Philadelphia, and a loss against Eddie Lenny in Chester, Pennsylvania.

In June 1901, he fought Eddie Lenny again, falling in the ninth round and cutting his cheek. He tried to rise but was advised to take the count. And for some time afterward, he was "very groggy." He then lost to Biz Mackey in Ohio and drew with Tim Callahan in Philadelphia.

Given the declining quality of his fighting, Dixon was likely drinking heavily and training little. At the same time he spent his money as fast as he earned it, and he found himself, again and again, with no choice but to return to the ring.

Unable now to get a good purse in the United States, Dixon decided he would leave America. He travelled by boat to England on July 16, 1902. The move left many believing that George had finally retired. In August 1902, the *Fort Wayne Morning Journal* announced, "Dixon to Leave the Prize Ring." The article said Dixon was to retire, "and it is about time that he did so." It noted that he had a career "equaled by few in his class" but that he had stayed in the ring too long. "Had he retired three years ago, he would have been spared the humiliation of defeats by McGovern, Young Corbett, and others, and his reputation would have been correspondingly better." Dixon's career was reviewed in the article, which claimed Dixon had fought in more than four hundred bouts and that he had earned more than $250,000. According to the paper, Dixon left for England because he had been hired by The Black Bass Athletic Club as a boxing instructor.

And though unclear, it seems that Dixon's move to England signalled the end of his relationship with manager Tom O'Rourke and with his wife Kitty.

* * *

In January 1902, a performance of *Uncle Tom's Cabin* took place at the Academy of Music in Chelsea, Massachusetts. The house was packed. The audience had come to watch the former heavyweight champion John L. Sullivan play the role of Simon Legree. And "spurred by the plaudits of the excited spectators, John L. acted as an actor never acted before." Sullivan, it was said, worked up to the climax of the story where Legree whips Uncle Tom "to within an inch of his life." Sullivan stepped into the role. "He wound his 10-foot lash around the writhing form of Uncle Tom to such good purpose that the actor playing the part screamed in agony, and finally fell fainting to the stage. There were loud protests from the audience and several women screamed and wept. Sullivan in his artistic fury forgot that the waist that was protected by the leather belt was the proper place to lick, and he licked Uncle Tom all over the body and legs, anywhere the whip happened to land. It was great acting, but one man thought it was a tough way of earning a modest stipend.

"Legree's death was another masterful impressionist picture. Sullivan is stout these days – downright fat, in fact – and he was puffing somewhat from previous exertions by the time for him to give up the ghost. Accordingly, when the fatal shot was fired, he fell to the stage all right, but as he wriggled his last wriggle, his breath came shorter and shorter – as was right and natural, seeing that he was dying. Some ribald youngster up in the gallery, however, who had no appreciation of the finer points of art, laughed joyously at the spectacle. It never touched him. Not for a minute. [Sullivan] calmly raised himself on one elbow and shot at him a cold and reproving glance. Of course, he subsided into awed silence before John L.'s glassy eye, and the death proceeded in proper fashion."

* * *

In England, George Dixon was chronically short of money and unable to stay away from drinking. So he stepped back into the ring. On December 28, 1902, *The Boston Globe* reported, "Dixon is Rich Again." The article indicated that since Dixon had arrived in England a year earlier, he had earned "nearly $7,000." Interviewed by a local journalist, Dixon talked about his good fortune. "I used to be a fool when I was younger and careless," said Dixon. "I never used to know the value of money. It was like nothing to me. But I have tasted the bitter pangs of poverty and know what it is to be hungry. I must have earned over $300,000 in my day, but I have little of this money left. I am taking excellent care of myself and will continue to do so. I am to fight Jem Bowker for the bantam championship of England on January 25. If I win everything will be fine. I will return to America, but not permanently. I have been well treated in England and expect to finish the rest of my days here."

Dixon was fighting at the rate of three or four bouts a month.

"Dixon Still in Fighting Game," ran a small headline in *The New York Times* on January 25, 1903. The article noted Dixon's upcoming fight with Jem Bowker. "Bowker," the paper reported, "is the present holder of the bantamweight championship." It also noted that "win or lose, this is to be Dixon's last fight in England before returning to the United States." The boxing record indicates that Dixon never did fight Bowker. And if the match had been arranged, it was cancelled.

On January 24, 1903, Dixon fought Jim Driscoll, a well-regarded Welsh featherweight.

Dixon lost in six rounds.

He did not return to the United States. Instead, he continued to fight in England for the next three years, fighting mostly unknown boxers, and rarely winning.

* * *

On November 6, 1904, *The Washington Post* published an article that focused on the financial lot of boxers, noting that many who had earned thousands of dollars in a short time soon found themselves without. George Dixon was offered as the first example. Tom O'Rourke was interviewed. "The money a champion prize fighter makes in the ring," said O'Rourke, "is a mere bagatelle to what he makes in the show business afterward." The newspaper argued that, "like a popular ward politician," a popular prizefighter "must spend money." The habits of George Dixon, John L. Sullivan, Jack Johnson, and Jim Jeffries all established the model for the champion boxer outside of the ring.

It was said that Jim Corbett "made and spent more money in the year following his fight with Sullivan than Sullivan made in his entire career as a fighter." Of course, Sullivan lost his title before the big money had entered the fight game. Sullivan often earned little more than $500 for a major bout. But just a few years later, "Corbett got $1,000 a week for forty weeks." Of Sullivan, it was still said that he had made perhaps $250,000, though it was just a third of what Corbett made in far less time. It also noted that Sullivan's "saloon in Boston was profitable until he became his own best customer at the bar."

The article also noted that "it is the same with the little fellows" like Dixon. Dixon was much like Corbett, reported the article. "He spends money faster than he earns it. No luxury is too costly for him if he wants it badly enough." Tom O'Rourke, it was said, tried to take care of Dixon's money after a fight, or Dixon would have "spent it at the rate of $500 every twenty-four hours. In upper Broadway it was a standing joke for weeks after a fight to see Dixon following O'Rourke around and begging for money. Sometimes the manager would keep him down to the car-fare point. If Dixon became too importunate, O'Rourke would feign annoyance and offer to give the little pugilist all his money in a lump. Then Dixon sheered off. He is sensible enough to know his weakness."

In late December 1904, *The Trenton Times* ran an article with the headline: "George Dixon Unheard Of – Very little is heard nowadays of George Dixon. He is in England and although he fights as often as twice a month the results of these contests rarely reach this side of the Atlantic."

In April 1905 there came further reports of Dixon's financial difficulties. British fighter Owen Moran, travelling in the United States, told the *New York Tribune* that Dixon had only earned $50 for his recent fight with Cockey Cohen.

"George Dixon is a Pauper," announced a small *Tribun*e headline in late April. "The little colored featherweight fighter, who has won thousands of dollars in the ring during many years that he has been engaged in fighting, is broke in England and unable to get enough money to get back to the country."

The Boston Globe reported on Dixon in June 1905. "George Dixon, the ex-featherweight champion of the world and undoubtedly the most popular colored boxer that ever stepped into a ring, is not in such sore straights in England as many of his former admirers believe," noted the article. It went on to say that Dixon now made his home in England, but he "is a suggestion of his former greatness," though he was in great demand among English fighters. And though he was making a regular income, he was having financial difficulties. "Time was," added the paper, "when the Boston colored lad would turn aside with scorn the offers he now accepts, but Dixon was always a sensible little chap and now that he realizes that he will never again regain the speed, cleverness and hitting power which brought to himself and Tom O'Rourke fame and fortune, he is far-sighted enough to accept about everything in the boxing line and he is consequently much better off than many of the top-notch boys in this country who lay claim to championship honors."

Dixon was in fact "living quietly in England" but had also travelled to Scotland "and the continent" where he was "accorded a royal welcome, for [his] fame as a boxer had long preceded him." The article noted that there had been rumours that Dixon had been financially stranded.

A friend who had received a letter from Dixon said, "[H]e is doing fairly well and is satisfied with the treatment he is receiving in England. However, he anticipates making a trip to Australia, as he believes he can win a lot of money by defeating the best little fellows in the Antipodes." The Lowell *Daily Sun* also reported that Dixon was "without a cent." Dixon was "at the end of his rope," living "hand to mouth" in London for months.

In July 1905, featherweight boxing great Abe Attell offered George Dixon his highest compliment. He said, "I learned more about boxing by watching the negro box Young Corbett and by then boxing Dixon myself than I have learned in all my fights combined."

A month later, in late August 1905, *The Boston Globe* reported that Dixon "had gone broke" in England. Congressman Timothy D. Sullivan was touring England when he became aware of Dixon's state. He found him in London. "George," he said, handing him money, "your tickets are ready any time you want to go home." Dixon must have agreed quickly, as Sullivan "immediately provided for his return."

Back in Boston, Dixon visited old friends, and he arranged a bout with Tommy Murphy in Philadelphia. Whether he reunited with Kitty is not known, but perhaps hoping to recapture old glory, he rehired Tom O'Rourke to act as his manager. The reunion must have been bittersweet. O'Rourke saw that Dixon was nothing like his former self, but his loyalty partly blinded him. In the end, the fight with Harlem Tommy Murphy lasted just two rounds. Dixon was knocked out by a "left swing to the solar plexus."

The following morning, in September 1905, *The Boston Globe* reported on the steadfast popularity of Dixon. "The popularity of Dixon was never better attested than tonight." A large crowd "had turned out to see Dixon in the ring." Upon climbing through the ropes, Dixon was greeted by thunderous applause and raucous cheers. Many of the fans reached through the ropes to shake his hand.

In December 1905, Dixon fought Frankie Howe in New York. When he entered the ring, he was "given a great reception." As *The New York Times* reported, "Dixon continues to retain his popularity. Though he has been in the game for practically a generation, he can yet put up a better bout than some of the alleged champions from the Hub, who have gone to New York with a great sound of timbrels."

At the same time, *The Trenton Times* reported, "Little Chocolate Has Lost Punch." The once great George Dixon, "who used to mow them all down not so very long ago, appeared before a local crowd at the Long Acre Athletic Club 158 West Twenty-ninth Street last night in a three-round bout with Frankie Howe of Chicago." Dixon had received a warm ovation when he entered the ring, and he managed at times to show something of his old self, keeping the nineteen-year-old Howie from hitting him. But, despite the warm encouragement from the crowd, the lacklustre fight ended in a draw.

That winter, Dixon travelled back to England where he drew against Pasty Haley and against Billy Ryan, both fighters of little reputation. Unable to earn a worthwhile purse in England, he returned home for good.

* * *

In January 1906, *The Logansport Daily Pharos* reported on a unique religious revival in New York City. In the early evening of January 10, five hundred "sporting men" sat at the ringside of the Long Acre Athletic Club listening "to a novelty in the form of a sermon preached between two bouts by William Asher, the evangelist from the west, who, with his wife, is holding saloon revivals in New York City."

The sight was unique to anyone's memory. After a bruising first bout, Asher, a small, wiry man with piercing eyes, made his way through the crowd and into the ring. The sporting men looked on suspiciously. Many "kept their hats on" and most continued to smoke. Asher just smiled and shook hands with men near the ring. "Don't worry," he joked loudly. "I won't touch you for your watch." His comment elicited some laughter. Then Asher turned serious and delivered a sermon derived from Timothy 6:12 – "Fight the good fight of the faith." With a Bible in his hand, Asher began to talk. "As a boy," he said, "I was fond of boxing, and even today I believe it a manly sport. But look at poor old John L. and our friend in the corner over there, George Dixon." Asher pointed, and the crowd turned and looked. When they recognized Dixon, they applauded.

"They have stowed away and lost lots of 'dough'," continued Asher, "and who of them would not today give back all his coin if he could be a healthy man again?" Asher talked of life's hardships and challenges in the metaphors of jabs, uppercuts, and swings. All the while, he punched the air to emphasize his points. "Well, boys," he said, "it's the same in religion. There isn't a bruiser among you, nor a chap on the face of the earth, who wouldn't give all he had if he could get a decision giving him religion. Lots of you fellows have taken the count lots of times, but how many of you ever stop to think what will happen when God gets the count on you. Look out for that day, boys, or it will be a sorry one for you."

Some in the crowd nodded.

"Boys," said Asher as he finished, "I like to see a good scrap, and I'm going to stay here until the last man is punched. Then I'll go home. God bless all of you." Asher left the ring, and the audience of hardened "sports" cheered. Then the bell for the next bout was rung.

What Dixon may have thought is not known.

* * *

In March 1906, *Police Gazette* sporting editor Sam Austin ran into George Dixon while he "was taking a chair in a boxing club uptown." Austin had long been a fan and supporter of Dixon and was most pleased to see him.

"Say," Dixon said to Austin after they shook hands, "have you got one of those old books you wrote about 'Black Champions?'"

"Yes," replied Austin, "what do you want it for?"

Dixon offered a smile. "Oh," he said, "I just want to read about what a fighter I used to be. From the way I've been doing lately, I find it difficult to believe that I ever knew anything about it."

When Austin wrote about the incident later, he noted, "... and this from the greatest little prize fighting machine the world ever saw."

Round Eleven

Swinging Blow Behind the Back: One of the most scientific as well as one of the prettiest and most effective blows I know of is the 'Swinging Behind the Back' blow. It is really a counter blow for a left hand body punch, but accomplished in such a manner that one scarcely realizes how it is landed. In the cut, which shows the blow, you will observe that my sparring companion has landed his left hand upon my body. He has also avoided a left hand blow aimed at his face by slipping his head to the right, but carelessly has pushed his head too far forward which gives me the opportunity to land with my right, by swinging behind my back. In cut No. 3, which shows the left hand blow, I warned my readers not to push the head too far forward. You now see why the head should be kept just beyond your opponent's left elbow.
    – George Dixon, "A Lesson in Boxing" (1893)

In the summer of 1906, George Dixon was asked to make a fight film for the American Mutoscope and Biograph Company. Fight films earned huge windfalls for big-name boxers by showing championship bouts around the country. And though Dixon was well past his prime, the producers thought there might be a few dollars in the project. As always, Dixon needed the cash, so he accepted the offer. One wonders, too, if he perhaps wanted some visual record of his work in the ring. In either case, the film producers induced him to put on the gloves for a three-minute, two-round film.

From the set position of the camera, the bout was staged in a ring no bigger than ten feet by ten feet. Behind the ring, on two sides, ran two rows of live spectators. All were men, most in dark suits and bowler hats. A few wore long mustaches. All were white. Behind these men ran another two rows of painted spectators. The painted spectators were similar in appearance to the live fans, presumably to give the film a greater sense of depth and realism.

In the opening moments of the fight film, an emcee stands in the centre of the ring. He wears a long jacket, tie, and dress pants. Though a silent film, he briefly addresses the cameraman then announces the fighters. Behind him, in the centre of the ring, lie two sets of leather gloves. The emcee raises his right hand to the far corner, and introduces Dixon's opponent, Chester Leon, an unknown fighter with no professional record. Leon, wearing light trunks, nimbly jumps through the ropes and takes his seat on a stool. He is followed into the ring by two handlers, both wearing white shirts, suspenders, and dark pants.

The emcee then raises his left hand to the near corner where Dixon appears. His back is to the camera. He wears dark trunks and a white belt. His handler also enters. He, too, wears a white shirt and black pants held up by suspenders, and his black hair is parted neatly down the middle.

Both Leon and Dixon take their seats. Towels are laid on their shoulders, and leather gloves are tied onto their hands. A referee replaces the emcee in the ring. He wears a white shirt and black tails. He nods at the audience, and then, while the fighters are prepared, he tests the ropes. After this, he invites the fighters to meet in the centre and offers instructions.

The two fighters are mirror images – both are the same height and are thin, muscular, and agile. They nod at the referee, shake hands with each other, and return to their respective corners. The seconds leave the ring.

A bell sounds to start the bout.

The two fighters approach, their heads back, their gloves up. Each uses a high front step before delivering a blow. They close in and exchange punches. But the blows are not crisp or well delivered. Instead, they are roundhouse punches that give the fight the feel of a street brawl or schoolyard scrap rather than a professional boxing match. Dixon throws alternating lefts and rights, before clinching, breaking away, and starting the looping punches again. Leon proves little better, mostly ducking beneath Dixon's blows and leaning into a clinch. When the film is stopped on a single frame, Dixon still appears impressive physically. But in motion, his movements are slow, and he is flat-footed.

After a few seconds more, following a flurry of wild, roundhouse swings by both fighters, Leon is suddenly down. At first, it appears that Leon was struck by a lightning fast blow, but when the film is rewound and reviewed slowly, it is clear that Leon took a dive.

No doubt, the dive was scripted for the film, a staged hint of Dixon at the height of his powers. Leon stays down for a count of six then rises. The fight continues. The two pugilists dance slowly around the ring, exchanging more looping punches that rarely connect.

The film then cuts to what appears to be the end of the round. After a few moments on the corner stools, the seconds leave the ring, and the fighters stand ready for round two. Dixon seems sharper now, perhaps finding some of the old magic in the rhythm of the movement. He dodges punches, delivers combinations, and pushes Leon back into the ropes. Yet the punches lack bite, perhaps by design or by agreement.

Then, almost suddenly, the fight ends.

The two shake hands and the referee sends each fighter to his respective corner. Dixon turns and looks for a moment in the direction of the camera. When the film is stopped in that moment, Dixon's face looks weary and older than his thirty-six years. Then, when the film starts again, the image of the two fighters cuts abruptly to black.

It's over.

The three minutes of film are a sad cinematic final word on Dixon's career.

And, in a sense, the fighter in the film was already dead.

* * *

Of George Dixon's last professional fight in 1906, no written account remains. Perhaps this is just as well. It was a sad conclusion to an extraordinary career, a final forgotten bout for a once great fighter, a fighter whose every round in the ring as champion had been described in rapturous detail.

His last fight came on December 10, 1906, against an unknown fighter from Rhode Island. His name was Monk The Newsboy. Monk The Newsboy fought in only twelve professional fights, of which Dixon was his tenth. He brought with him a record of three losses, three wins, and three draws when he entered the ring with Dixon in Providence, Rhode Island, at the Lymansville

Athletic Club. The fight lasted fifteen uneventful rounds, after which Monk The Newsboy was declared the winner. The loss for Dixon must have been decisive.

It is impossible to know what may have been going through Dixon's mind in the dressing room after the fight. But after nearly a thousand professional fights, and after winning championships in three weight classes, George Dixon, one of the greatest boxers ever to enter the ring, finally hung his leather gloves on the hook by the door for the last time. He left the dressing room with his bag on his shoulder and never returned as a professional fighter.

Officially, George Dixon fought in 150 matches, winning 69 (with 38 knockouts), losing 29, and drawing 52. In truth, however, an accurate count of his fights in the ring would be far higher. The *Police Gazette* reported that Dixon had fought in more than a thousand bouts, but this is almost certainly a tabloid exaggeration. Still, Tom O'Rourke claimed that Dixon fought in more than eight hundred bouts, which seems plausible. If true, hardly a week went by in George Dixon's twenty-year career as a boxer when he did not enter the ring.

It was then, and still remains, an unparalleled accomplishment.

* * *

Not long after Dixon hung up his gloves, John L. Sullivan happened across him. Dixon was begging for money in the streets of New York. Sullivan was genuinely happy to see George and the two chatted about old times.

"I've blown my luck," Dixon finally told Sullivan.

"So did I once," John L. offered in return. He reached into his pocket, retrieved what money he had and handed it to Dixon. "But I cut out the drink, and I've got it all back."

Dixon took the money and nodded. "I'm afraid it's too late to shift now," he said. "I know I'm all in and that the end is near."

John L. Sullivan put his hand on George Dixon's shoulder, nodded in understanding, and they parted company for the last time.

* * *

In January 1907, *The Post-Standard* of Syracuse, New York, wrote, "George Dixon refuses to stop fighting or, rather, he is compelled to keep on fighting. The thousands of dollars that Dixon earned in the ring were all squandered in riotous living, and George must fight to keep alive. Dixon does not remember how he squandered the money. In fact, his ideas as to how his finances dwindled are very hazy." Whether this article referred to the December fight with Monk The Newsboy or whether Dixon was fighting in other unrecorded exhibitions for what money he could get is uncertain. But given that his survival still rested on his fists, it is hard not to think that he engaged in some backroom bouts for a few dollars.

Six months later, a *New York Tribune* article ran under the headline, "George Dixon Down and Out." Dixon had attended a benefit for Terry McGovern, who himself had fallen on hard times, becoming "demented." During the evening at Madison Square Garden, Dixon slipped into the dressing room of boxer Harry Harris and asked for "10 cents for the cab fare home." He explained to Harris that he was "flat broke and without a hint as to where his breakfast was to come from."

Harris was moved by Dixon's plea and handed him a five-dollar bill. Then, leaving his dressing room, he went into the crowd and shared what he had just learned with men he knew. The "sports" quickly assembled and began to gather money. So, too, the group, which had been auctioning cartoons by New York artists, auctioned one particular cartoon for Dixon. A "Wall Street Broker secured it at $1,100." In another ten minutes, an additional $400 was added to the total. The money was then placed "in the hands of a committee with instructions to dole it out to Dixon at the rate of $25 a week."

The next day, *The Trenton Times* also ran a short piece under the headline, "George Dixon is a Wreck – George Dixon is a physical wreck. When the former feather-weight champion put up his hands in an exhibition at the McGovern benefit, expressions of pity were heard on all sides. The little fellow does not weigh more than 110 pounds and his movements in the ring indicated extreme weakness. He went on to help McGovern in the hour of need without a dollar in his pocket, but when he left the Garden, he had nearly $600, the result of the generosity of old admirers. Dixon's plight was a matter of general surprise. He blew a fortune in his palmy days."

In November 1907, the *San Antonio Light* noted, "George Dixon, the former featherweight champion, who is now said to be practically 'down and out,' has received an offer from Joe Gans to serve in his new hotel [in Baltimore], which he is building. Gans, who is now on a tour of Minnesota and other northern states, wants Dixon to take charge of the bar in the establishment. The hostelry will be called 'The Goldfield' in honor of the Nevada town in which Gans defeated [Oscar 'Battling'] Nelson."

Unfortunately, for reasons never made clear, the arrangements for Dixon to take over the bar fell through.

In mid-December 1907, George Dixon spoke with a sports reporter from the *Evening World*. The reporter found him near a saloon in New York. He asked how he was doing.

"I was a foolish boy," said Dixon. "I spent or gave away all I got. But I don't see any of the people I helped willing to do much for me. The only people who stand by me at all now are the people I never did anything for."

The reporter noted that Dixon "had drifted into the tide of homeless wrecks that swirl around dark corners and deserted lonely places. Men who used to know him pulled their hats over their eyes and hurried by when they saw him. Toward the end, it must have seemed to Little Chocolate that every one he met was hurrying by."

Another sports reporter from the *San Jose Evening News* also remembered seeing George Dixon about this time. "One night I shall never forget," the reporter recalled, "[was] a dreary, cold, rainy night on [the street]. After the pub was closed, the crowds were winding their way home through the drizzle. Little George Dixon stood alone on the corner, tears streaming down his cheeks. He seemed to be fighting some imaginary opponent. Even then, his movements, as he engaged his phantom foe, were the poetry of motion."

This fight would be Dixon's last.

Round Twelve

The Knock Out Blow: *Every person who goes to see or reads about boxing matches is familiar with the 'knock out' blow. It has caused many a dollar to change hands. It has also caused many an ambitious young athlete who aspired to championship honors and whose name was gradually ascending the ladder to fame and fortune to sink into oblivion. The 'knock out' blow gained its first prominence through John L. Sullivan. There are many ways of landing the blow but the one most practiced is the straight right hand punch on the point of the jaw. To land a 'knock out' blow, carefully gauge your opponent's distance and just keep out of reach of his right hand by about an inch. Then draw him on to swing his right at your head. The moment he leads just draw your head back and his arm will pass your head. When the arm goes by your head, then hit out straight from the shoulder with your right for the middle or point of his jaw. In case your opponent should strike straight with his right instead of swinging the blow, jump back and then slip to the side, out of the way.*
    — George Dixon, "A Lesson in Boxing" (1893)

During the afternoon of January 6, 1908, as George Dixon lay alone in his Bellevue Hospital bed, Dr. Hooker paid him a visit. The two sat in silence for some time, until Dixon finally spoke. "I'm down for the count, doctor," he said. "I know it."

Dr. Hooker put a hand on Dixon's shoulder and said nothing.

"I'm licked," added Dixon, "and booze did it." Dixon turned his head away, his "teeth clenched tightly together, but without a murmur, even from the terrible pain." Throughout the next hour, George Dixon lay in silence. No doubt he was conscious of Dr. Hooker still sitting beside him, and conscious, too, of his life slipping away. Then, just before 2:00 p.m., Dixon took a deep breath and looked to the ceiling. He exhaled slowly.

Dr. Hooker watched in silence.

A moment later, George Dixon was dead.

* * *

Across North America and England, hundreds of newspapers ran obituaries of George Dixon. Some were ridiculous, offering their remembrances in strained prose. "After losing several battles in the ring with third-rate opponents and fighting a long-distance battle with King Alcohol," ran one, "George Dixon, one of the greatest fighters the world ever saw, was finally counted out by the great referee yesterday at the Bellevue Hospital in New York."

Others were heart-wrenchingly sublime. "Drink Ends Dixon's Life," began the obituary in *The Washington Times*. "The greatest fighter of his time and the winner of several hundred fistic encounters, George Dixon, the negro pugilist, familiarly called 'Little Chocolate,' died today in the alcoholic ward of Bellevue Hospital, a victim of a long fight with drink. Idolized in his prime by thousands as a pugilistic hero, George Dixon passed away practically penniless and without friends. Dixon was thirty-seven years old, and for many years held the title of featherweight champion. George Dixon fought several hundred ring battles, his first being in 1886, when he whipped a boy named Johnson in Halifax, N.S. From that time, until Terry McGovern knocked him out in 1900 and broke his heart, no man of his weight ever whipped him.

"He won the feather-weight title in 1891 by whipping the champion, Cal McCarthy. Dixon was a perfect fighting machine, so far as attack and defense was concerned, and his peculiar ability to strike a blow from any position made him a formidable opponent. Dixon won thousands of dollars in the prize ring, which he spent with convivial companions. A wasted, wane figure was brought to Bellevue Hospital two days ago and ticketed in the alcoholic ward as George Dixon. To the doctor he said that he had 'fought his last fight with John Barleycorn and had been beaten.' He told the physicians that he had no friends except John L. Sullivan. His condition grew rapidly worse, and late to-day the former champion died."

The outpouring of affection for George Dixon from all quarters was overwhelming. In life, and now in death, George Dixon transcended the racism of the age by touching the dignity and humanity in everyone he came across.

* * *

After Dixon passed away, his body was brought to the Long Acre Athletic Club, where he had fought so many fights. There, his body was laid in the centre ring for viewing. More than a thousand people gathered in the chairs surrounding the ring to pay their final respects. Two ministers – one white, the other black – entered the ring and offered their reflections.

Later, the coffin was brought to the railway station in New York where it was loaded into a boxcar and covered in flowers. "Dixon's fate had been the principal topic of conversation in sporting circles in New York since his death," reported *The Desert News* of Salt Lake City. "The little fighter, who for twelve years held the championship title in his class, made a fortune during his days in the ring, but he promptly squandered every cent of it and when through dissipation his days in the ring were ended, he drifted lower and lower until he became a wanderer and almost a vagrant. Those who profited by his free-handedness in his days of prosperity refused to help him in his days of adversity, nor were they among those who contributed to the fund for his burial or who sent the flowers that covered the coffin."

On the morning of January 9, 1908, the train that carried George Dixon's casket from New York arrived in Boston, where relatives and friends waited. By the afternoon, a crowd of more than two thousand men and women, black and white, gathered inside the African Methodist Episcopal Church, on the corner of Charles and Mount Vernon Streets in Boston, for a service to remember Dixon. The swelling numbers of mourners waiting to pay their last respects were so great that the modest church could not accommodate them all. "Unquestionably," wrote the reporter for the *Providence Evening Tribune*, "no other funeral of a colored person ever held in this city was so well attended."

For much of the day, Dixon's body lay in the chapel of Hutchins's Funeral Home on Shawmut Avenue, where hundreds were said to have viewed the body. In the late afternoon, the casket was then closed and delivered to the home of George's brother, James, who lived at 20 Grove Street in the west end of the city. There, members of the family and friends continued their visitation.

The next day, on January 10, 1908, the body was moved by pallbearers Joe Walcott, John E. Butler, Edward Day, Spencer Riley, James Harris, and Edward Martin and placed in a hearse that drove to the African Methodist Episcopal Church for the final service. At 2:00 p.m., the casket arrived inside the church and was met at the head of the aisle by Rev. T.W. Henderson, the pastor, Rev. E.L. Bell of Chelsea, Rev. Dr. Duckery of Cambridge, Rev. Dr. Harold of Cambridge, and Rev. H.J. Callis of Zion's Church.

A Mrs. Hutchins played Beethoven's funeral march on the organ, as the clergymen escorted the body to the front of the pulpit. A women's quartet offered a hymn, and then, appropriately, Rev. Callis read from the fourteenth chapter of Job. "Man that is born of a woman is of few days and full of trouble," he read aloud. "He cometh forth like a flower, and is cut down; he fleeth also as a shadow, and continueth not ..."

Rev. Harold offered a prayer, and a woman named Mrs. Gilbert Harris sang a song. The pastor then preached the funeral sermon, taking his text from Hebrews, chapter nine, verse 27: "It is appointed unto man once to die, but after this is the judgment." Later, with words lost to time, the pastor gave the eulogy. One can easily imagine his thoughts about George Dixon reflecting the challenges of Job.

Afterward the committal service was given, and Rev. Bell offered the benediction. Finally, amid the sounds of crying, the casket was opened so the body could be viewed. In all, it was reported that more than five thousand people passed by the body of the former champion.

Just before 4:00 p.m., the casket was closed for the last time. The clergymen escorted the body down the aisle, where the pallbearers lifted the casket to the waiting hearse. Soon afterward, the hearse left the church with ten carriages carrying George's admirers and family following behind. The procession made its slow progress south, through the winding streets, in the cool of the winter's evening, to the temporary resting place near the cemetery, until the spring ground could receive the body of George Dixon.

* * *

In March 1908, *The Anaconda Standard* reported that plans were being made for Memorial Day, 1908, when "a $1,500 popular subscription monument will be erected to the memory of George Dixon, the late boxing champion. The striking feature of this lasting tribute will be a bronze figure of Dixon of heroic proportions. The statue will be 6 feet 6 inches in height, will be of bronze, and will represent Dixon in costume, standing erect with one hand resting on his hip, the other hanging at his side. The base of the statue will be a block of perfect granite, six feet square and of similar height. In addition a lot has been purchased in Mount Hope cemetery, 7 by 13 feet, at the corner of Maple and Lake avenues. Dixon's body will be removed to this lot early in the spring with the exercises in connection with the unveiling of the monument on Memorial Day, if the present plans are carried out."

* * *

In the early spring, a solemn procession followed the casket of George Dixon to Mount Hope Cemetery in Mattapan, near Boston. By the time the body arrived at the cemetery, a quiet darkness had fallen. The procession entered the grounds, passing the stone gateposts, and ambled along a half-mile of path before stopping at an area of new burial ground just across from a large pond. While lanterns were lit around the gravesite, the coffin was lifted from the hearse and placed on the ground. No doubt the lantern light played softly on the numerous floral tributes as final words were offered and the coffin containing George Dixon's remains was lowered into the open earth.

Some time later, a pink granite stone was placed above George's grave. On its polished face was a relief carving – a life-like bust of George Dixon. Even after a hundred years, the stone remains a simple yet striking memorial.

Beneath the bust is written "George E. Dixon, July 29, 1870 – January 6, 1908."

* * *

What John L. Sullivan thought of Dixon's passing is uncertain, though he no doubt felt a deep sense of loss. George Dixon was a friend who understood his own experiences like no other. It is fitting then that Sullivan, who died in 1918, was buried not far from his friend, just across the street from Dixon, in Mattapan's Old Calvary Cemetery, beneath a stark, grey obelisk that simply bears the names of John L. Sullivan and his family members.

*   *   *

On August 29, 1908, *The Sun* newspaper reported that a memorial fountain for George Dixon had been erected on the corner of Thompson and Broome Streets in New York City. The committee that had first suggested a statue for Dixon's grave had instead decided that a "watering place" memorial would be a fitting tribute. Terry McGovern and Young Corbett were the "principal factors" in donating funds. The fountain was "one of the most beautiful of its kind in New York." The street side of the fountain was designed for horses, and the sidewalk side for public use. On the inside wall, surrounded by a wreath, were the words, "In memory of George Dixon. Erected by his friends, 1908."

The "watering place" monument stood for many years at the corner of Thompson and Broome streets, but over time, as such fountains for horses and the public became out of date, it was removed and discarded for scrap. Two photographs of the fountain remain in the Library of Congress. In one picture, the fountain sits on the sidewalk above a littered street, in front of a wall of advertising posters. Water spews from a lion's mouth into a large basin. In the other photograph, taken from the opposite side of the fountain, a row of tenement houses sits in the distance.

A sense of loneliness pervades each photograph.

After the Bell

Before closing my little book, I would like to add that I make no pretense of being an author, but found this little experiment an excellent evening pastime. Hoping I have pleased my reader, I am, very truly, GEORGE DIXON.
  – George Dixon, "A Lesson in Boxing" (1893)

For all the achievements and accolades George Dixon earned and received in his lifetime, it is surprising how quickly he was forgotten in the years following his death. As memory became history and the years slowly passed, only those boxing fans with an awareness of the sport's personalities remembered to place Dixon among the ever-changing lists of boxing's greatest. In 1955, Dixon was inducted into Canada's Sports Hall of Fame. He earned the same accolade in 1956 in the American Ring Hall of Fame. And in 1990, the International Boxing Hall of Fame formally recognized Dixon among boxing's greats.

Yet in Halifax, Nova Scotia, where the champion was born, George Dixon only occupies faint space in the city's memory, with a squat, brick community centre – coincidentally sitting in the same block between Gottingen and Brunswick streets where Letson's Lane may once have run – that bears his name. On the back wall of the Dixon Centre hangs a faded photo of George. Though nearby residents would likely recognize Dixon's name and may even recall that Dixon was a title-winning boxer, few would appreciate the full extent of George Dixon's accomplishments.

Even in the Nova Scotia Sports Hall of Fame, the organization dedicated to remembering sports greats from the province, George Dixon – arguably Nova Scotia's greatest athlete – warrants only a modest display.

So what, a hundred years since his death, is one to make of George Dixon's life?

Much, I think.

In the ring, George Dixon was among a select few who crafted what we have come to know as "the sweet science" of boxing. And he reached rarified heights that few pugilists have ever reached. More than this, he was a true artist of the age. Like modern dancer Isadora Duncan, George Dixon explored and pushed the artistic possibilities of athleticism. His art was boxing, plied on a twenty-four-square-foot canvas. And in that space, he created dazzling works of physicality in a medium that had astonishing metaphoric power.

So, too, George Dixon played a meaningful role in shaping the outer edges of the early civil rights movement for black Americans and black Canadians. Late in Dixon's career *The Boston Globe* offered a keen observation of Dixon's importance beyond his achievements in the ring. "To him belongs the credit of obliterating the strong prejudices against colored pugilists," noted the article. "No one better than himself knows how far-reaching was that prejudice. He was compelled at the outset to accept defeat and lose victories on account of it even in the city of his home. Rarely was it that a colored man was permitted to score a victory over a white man, even though the latter was far inferior. The last battle he had in Boston, before going under the management of Tom O'Rourke, illustrates the antagonism there was to him. He knocked out his opponent, a popular white boxer, and the referee, heeding the cries of the spectators, declared the contest a draw, saying it was not right to give a colored man an award over a white man. Those of that crowd of spectators who are now alive are Dixon's friends and would resent vigorously any attempt to rob him of a victory fairly won."

Even in a fragmented form, the story of George Dixon's rise and fall is deeply moving. It is moving because, though few of us have actually stepped into a boxing ring, we all implicitly understand the nature of the fight. We root for or against boxers like George Dixon not merely out of bloodlust – though therein lies much dark truth. Rather, we root for or against boxers like George Dixon because we recognize in their physical and artistic struggle our own fights, our own wins, and our own losses.

If boxing from the late nineteenth century through the late twentieth century reflects our most pointed struggles with class and race, then George Dixon was among our greatest boxers not just because of his extraordinary fights, but because his fights poignantly reflected, in metaphoric form, our collective struggles. George Dixon spent his short life fighting to rise above these collective struggles, to win these fights on sheer talent and will.

And for a time, he did.